The Magic Pencil

Published by
Peachtree Publishers, Ltd.
494 Armour Circle, N.E.
Atlanta, Georgia 30324

Design and illustrations by Paulette L. Lambert

10 9 8 7 6 5 4 3 2 1

Manufactured in the United States of America

ISBN 0-934601-52-6

Library of Congress Catalog Card Number 88-60420

The Magic Pencil

Teaching Children Creative Writing

A Workbook For Parents And Teachers

EVE SHELNUTT

Illustrations by PAULETTE L. LAMBERT

Peachtree Publishers, Ltd.

Contents

Introduction, 4

A Few Words About Supplies, 10

Working with Very Young Children, 13

What to Do When Children Make Errors in Writing, 15

Exercises to Motivate Young Writers — Even Reluctant Ones, 16

Solving a Writing Problem, 19

Part One
Learning Through Play with Language

Introduction, 22

Contents, 23
  1. All About Me, 24
  2. All About My Home, 26
  3. All About My Street, 27
  4. All About My Town, 28
  5. A Book About Me, 30
  6. Publication of *A Book About Me*, 32
  7. The Diary of an Imaginary Person, 34
  8. Drawing a Map of the Land Where the Imaginary Person Lives, 36
  9. Writing Stories and Poems About the Imaginary Person, 38
  10. Producing a Book from the Stories and Poems About the Imaginary Person, 40
  11. Variations on Keeping a Diary of an Imaginary Person, 42
  12. Stories from an Imaginary Town, 44
  13. Disaster Strikes City X, 48
  14. Fact-Finding Trips, 49
  15. Recording Personal Histories, 50
  16. Letters to and from an Imaginary Pen Pal, 51
  17. Variations on the "Letters to and from an Imaginary Pen Pal" Exercise, 53
  18. Changing a Story into a Play, 54
  19. Changing a Poem into a Story, 57
  20. Changing a Story into a Poem, 58

Part Two
A Focus on Skills

Introduction, 62

Contents, 63

  1. Making Writing Visual: The Simile, 64
     a. A Poem Using Similes, 64
     b. Revising Written Work: Adding Similes, 65
     c. The Silly-Simile Game, 67
     d. Similes to Express Strong Feelings, 68
  2. Turning the Simile into a Metaphor, 70
  3. Stories That Begin with Metaphors, 72
  4. Metaphor as Disguise, 73
  5. Developing Contemplation in a Young Writer, 74
  6. Revision After Contemplation, 77
  7. Metaphorical Writing Following a Trip, 78
  8. What Is Poetry?, 80
  9. A Book About Poetry, 81
  10. Helping Young Writers Correct Errors, 83
  11. Learning to Organize from Activity, 86
  12. From Letters to Essays, 88
  13. The Writer Becomes an Editor, 90
  14. Methods of Research, 92
  15. Making Stories More Complete, 94
  16. Research by Interviewing, 96
  17. Writing an Essay from an Interview, 98
  18. The Reader or Audience for Writing, 100
  19. Concrete Poetry, 101
  20. Vocabulary-Building Simile Poem Using Synonyms, 102
  21. Words Reveal How We Feel, 104
  22. Giving a Story's Main Character Personality, 105
  23. Writing Stimulated by Writing and Combined with Revision, 108
  24. What Happens When I Write?, 109
  25. Talking to the Author, 111
  26. Brainstorming, 112

Reading List, 117
A Guide for School Teachers, 121
Afterword, 127

Introduction

This book is for anyone interested in helping children learn how to write. Its basic premise is that children who *enjoy* writing learn to write more skillfully than children who dislike writing.

Before I began to write *The Magic Pencil*, I thought often about a six-year-old I once taught. At The Writing School in Dayton, Ohio, an after-school enrichment program in creative writing, I took a class of first-graders to the Dayton Museum of Art one rainy Friday in October.

Alicia, a slight, shy girl who rarely talked and definitely didn't like to write, walked through the museum saying nothing all afternoon except "Oh!"

She would turn from one painting or sculpture to another, take a deep breath while squeezing my hand, and then her normally soft voice would almost explode: "Oh!"

When coming to The Writing School, Alicia normally hung back at the door until the activity of other children would make her arrival less noticeable. But on the Monday following our trip to the museum, Alicia burst into the room, grabbed my skirt, pulled me closer, and whispered, "We went to the Mus-e-um!"

Yes, I know, I said, and we'll go again.

But I had it wrong. "No!" said Alicia, nearly shouting this time. "My *momma* took me. And *she* said it was bea-u-ti-ful!"

Over time I heard (and read) a lot about Alicia's mother, who had three other small children whose lives she was enriching. She, too, was shy and not at all sure about this thing Alicia was coming to The Writing School to study—creative writing?

"And *she* said we can go *every Saturday*!" Alicia shouted.

Her mother began to appear often in Alicia's writing—suddenly, it seemed, Alicia was bursting with stories and poems she wanted to write. And, as she had promised, her mother did take Alicia to the museum on Saturdays. Above all, she told Alicia that her *writing* was "bea-u-ti-ful!"

She became Alicia's writing teacher, although she did not, herself, like to write.

I couldn't have wanted a better teacher for Alicia. Simply

by listening and asking questions and exclaiming over Alicia's writing, she helped make writing a *natural* part of Alicia's day-to-day activity.

The Magic Pencil is, first and most importantly, about this kind of discovery between children and adults. It is really about kids teaching parents and other teachers *how* to teach writing, for this is what can happen.

We know that writing and reading are crucial to the development of academic skills. And we know that parents and educators are concerned because Johnny can neither read nor write very well.

After assessing the writing samples of fifty-five thousand eighth- and eleventh-graders in 1985, Archie Lapointe, executive director of the national Assessment of Educational Progress (a research project of the Educational Testing Service in Princeton, New Jersey), said, "Performance in writing in our schools is, quite simply, *bad*."

What *can* adults do to help children learn competence in writing?

We know that learning to communicate ideas and emotions through written language is not an easy process. We know that it is, in fact, a never-ending process of discovery.

But kids *want* to take on new and challenging tasks. Last summer I watched my neighbor's seven-year-old boy take the training wheels from his bike, wrestling awkwardly with his father's wrench as his four-year-old brother offered advice. And when the "babyish" training wheels were tossed to one side, the seven-year-old, who suddenly looked so small and vulnerable, began to wobble down the street on two wheels. Of course he fell and of course he picked himself up and began again. All day—with time out for lunch and patching up with a few bandages from his mother—he practiced, laughing sometimes, whimpering at others, and occasionally kicking the bike that seemed to have a mind of its own. But that evening we all gathered outside to watch the wonder: Kevin riding on two wheels down the street without one crashing fall. We clapped, Kevin grinned—it was quite a celebration.

A child can be equally triumphant about learning to

write—and with no scratches or bruises!

The Magic Pencil offers two integrated methods for guiding children to accept the challenges of writing. They are:

1. Help children make writing a natural part of their day-to-day lives.
2. Help children learn to move freely between academic writing and creative writing.

Academic writing, or the kind of writing normally associated with school—the writing of reports, term papers, essays, etc.—and what we term creative or personal writing, in which children focus on their imaginations and feelings, *can* be integrated writing processes. When this happens, children can come to feel that *they* are in charge of acts of communication: in some situations, they discover, logically organized, informational essays communicate ideas efficiently and clearly; in other situations, they discover that what they want to communicate deserves and requires a less linear, more indirect approach.

When kids enjoy writing and feel that *they* are in charge of their own writing processes, academic writing and creative writing become equally valued tools of expression.

Children who resist writing are probably children who have become confused about what's considered real. "Real" writing in school—academic writing—can seem frightening to children when response focuses on avoiding errors and putting aside personal feelings and imagination. Then, in an effort to be "correct" and to satisfy adult expectations, children begin to "solve" academic writing problems by: 1) narrowing the range of their writing until they can always make it correct; 2) avoiding creative thinking to decrease the possibility of error; 3) writing only imitatively to avoid error; and 4) blocking out feelings about language and material, again to prevent error.

And children seeking to satisfy adult requirements in academic writing by separating academic writing from creative or personal writing are confirmed in this separation when teachers (often the most progressive teachers) set up creative writing "corners." Creative writing becomes something that happens "over there," as a "reward" for completion of the "real" academic work. Progressive language arts coordinators often bring in visiting poets and storytellers from the "outside" to teach an occasional lesson in creative writing, thus underscoring the idea that imaginative writing happens "out there," an infrequent reward for or respite from "real" writing.

The Magic Pencil is designed to help children avoid this confusion. By using the exercises, children will learn to move freely between academic and creative writing by deciding themselves how *they* want to communicate. Instead of segregating writing into such categories as "school-writing," which children often learn to dislike, and "fun" writing, which children are often taught is unimportant, children will ask: Who will read my writing? What does my writing say to a reader? For the reader I have in mind, does the writing I have chosen communicate effectively? For the reader I have in mind, do I need to correct errors of grammar, spelling, and punctuation? In this piece of writing, do I want to focus on giving information, on conveying feelings, or a combination of the two?

Questions such as these, asked by *children* of their own writing, help children learn to take responsibility for their writing. And when children accept responsibility for their writing, what happens to them as writers is just what *teachers in schools* want young writers to experience:

1. a loss of fear about writing;
2. excitement about writing as a tool of communication;
3. confidence in writing as a process of self-discovery and discovery about the world;
4. involvement in writing as a process of revision, as what the child learns with each piece of writing helps him or her reevaluate previous writing.

The Design of *The Magic Pencil*

Following the introduction are sections about supplies and about working with very young children; a note about helping children understand the concept of errors in writing; and a set of exercises which can be used to motivate young writers, even reluctant ones.

Following these are a number of exercises which are designed to be used in sequence so that the child will build upon particular skills and concepts. These exercises are separated into two sections. Part I contains exercises designed to stimulate children's enthusiasm about writing and to help children discover a wealth of material for writing. Adults guiding children through these exercises will provide materials, present the ideas in the exercises, encourage children to participate in the writing process suggested in each exercise, and answer any of the children's questions that arise. Many children will want to work alone on the exercises in Part I with a minimum of adult interaction. Adults working with children who like to write independently will want to express interest in and appreciation of any writing the children show them. Other children will want more adult interaction. The child should guide the degree of interaction—this is a time for children to discover, to play, and to celebrate learning about writing. Be prepared to help, be prepared to step aside. And *never* criticize the young writer's efforts.

The exercises in Part II focus on specific skills. By this time, the young writer will be involved in expression through writing and will want to know more specifically how to shape and refine writing. This does not mean that the adult helping the child with the exercises in Part II needs to be a practiced writer.

Each exercise has a description of the specific skills the child will work on. The best writing teacher is not an authority on writing who "knows everything." For the exercises in Part II, the best approach is for the adult to say aloud, "Let's see: we'll read this exercise and decide together how to do it." It will help the child if the adult frequently asks the child, "What do *you* think we should do?"

Following the exercises in Part II is a list of books which both adults and children interested in writing will find useful. Children will be encouraged to consult these books or similar ones as they work on the exercises in Part II. Adults helping children learn to write can encourage children to use books as a tool in writing if the children *see* their adult teachers consulting books in order to answer questions about writing. In response to exercises in Part II, adults should feel free to ask a young writer to consult books which may be useful in doing a particular exercise.

Finally, *The Magic Pencil* contains a "postscript" specifically for teachers using the book in classrooms.

But How Much Time Does Using the Exercises Really Take?

At first, for several days as you gather materials for use in writing, it may seem that using the exercises will take a considerable amount of time. Soon you will discover that your child or group of children are gathering writing materials and beginning to generate excitement about writing projects. You will find a child's excitement "catching," and teaching will begin to seem not so much like teaching as like an exciting game of discovery. Many of the exercises encourage a child to work independently of any adult interaction except for an occasional exclamation of interest or pleasure over the child's writing. On some rainy days you may find it relaxing and pleasurable to sit with a child or group of children and play one of the "games" in Part I or II. Other exercises are very informal and easy to participate in with a child or group of children almost anywhere—in a car, on a school bus trip, etc.

And you won't need to spend time grading children's writing. The children using the exercises in the book will learn to correct their own writing. Teachers in schools who are required to grade students' writing will discover that grading becomes less of a task when children produce quantities of writing, revise it because they want to, and present the teacher with only their best writing.

Teaching children writing through use of *The Magic Pencil* will come to seem less like teaching and more like a mutual adventure between child and adult, a grand adventure in discovery about language. Don't all of us lose track of time when we're having fun? That is what *The Magic Pencil* is all about.

A Few Words About Supplies

If you are beginning the process of stimulating a child's interest, it is important to consider the child's current attitude toward writing before presenting the prospective writer with materials. A ten-year-old boy who is convinced that he "hates" to write will probably respond badly to being given a stack of paper and a box of pencils and being told they are for writing projects. On the other hand, he may respond well to the suggestion that he and his friends begin a newsletter focusing on sports in the neighborhood. You may find him *asking* for writing supplies!

On pages 16-19 you will find a list of writing activities appropriate for children who believe they don't enjoy writing or who fear failure when they write.

For children whose attitudes toward writing are either neutral or positive, the process of gathering materials can be an aid to learning and should involve the young writer. Accompany the child to an office supply store, if possible, and allow the child to help select supplies and observe the variety of available writing materials.

It is useful to have on hand such standard materials as:

1. reams of lined and unlined paper in a variety of sizes
2. pencils in a variety of colors, a set of colored felt-tip markers
3. nontoxic paste or glue
4. sheets of poster board in white and a variety of colors
5. construction paper in a variety of colors
6. Scotch tape, masking tape, strapping tape
7. a roll of butcher's paper or brown wrapping paper or sheets of newspaper
8. a number of pocket-sized spiral notebooks
9. several bound books of blank paper
10. envelopes in a variety of sizes
11. scissors with rounded ends
12. a dictionary
13. a thesaurus

14. an atlas, including maps of the world
15. a portable tape recorder and blank tapes
16. a number of folders with pockets for storing of writing
17. cardboard boxes for storing "junk"
18. old magazines, maps, books that can be cut apart.

Some of the writing activities listed in the book will require additional supplies. As a part of the prewriting activity, allow the child to help accumulate the required supplies and to keep them readily available. Writing projects can include prewriting activities which require space and permission for the child to create some disorder.

It is helpful to young writers to be given permission to be as "messy" as they need to be for the stimulation of imagination during a prewriting activity; it will also help the writer to focus on the actual writing project which follows the prewriting activity if the adult supervising the project urges the child to clear away material that may be distracting.

Try to observe a child writer closely enough to understand the degree of order or disorder that stimulates the imagination. A rigid adult focus on order during a writing activity can dampen a child's enthusiasm and trigger fear of failure since failure at writing is associated with "messy" papers in many a child's mind. And while writing supplies can be neatly stored, they should always be where a child can get to them quickly; the process of getting out materials and putting them away again should not be made tiresome to a child.

Apart from the supplies listed as standard materials for writing projects, additional materials to be used in prewriting activities can be accumulated by both the child and adult supervisor. You and the child need not know how these materials will be used in writing activities when gathering them. These materials should be gathered simply because they are themselves interesting objects. Having boxes of interesting objects accessible to young writers can be an aid in stimulating the child to invent his or her own writing projects. Materials which many children have found

stimulating in writing projects are:

1. color cards from paint stores
2. stones, leaves, acorns, sticks, small bottles of pond or sea water, bark from a variety of trees, containers of dirt from various parts of the country, etc.
3. a variety of wigs and masks, homemade or purchased
4. old clothing and accessories, especially jewelry, gloves, hats, scarves
5. old shoes in a variety of sizes and styles
6. paper bags in a variety of sizes
7. wall paper in many patterns
8. foreign language dictionaries
9. art books, *National Geographic* magazines, old photographs, preferably ones which can be cut into and/or written on
10. boxes in which refrigerators, stoves, freezers are shipped
11. old sheets which can be cut and torn
12. kitchen utensils and safe carpentry tools
13. stamps from foreign countries
14. ink pads and individual rubber letters used with stamp pads
15. miniature ceramic tiles
16. marbles in a variety of sizes
17. coins from foreign countries
18. heavy cardboard
19. pictures of birds and animals
20. a box of kosher salt or any heavy-grain salt
21. musical instruments: a harmonica, a kazoo, a comb and waxed paper, a xylophone, a drum, a tin penny whistle, etc.
22. rulers in a variety of lengths
23. "invisible" ink
24. bottles with lids.

All of the materials collected for writing activities should be safe and appropriate to the child's age and development.

Working with Very Young Children

Children can "write" long before they develop the manual dexterity to make letters. Here are some activities for preschoolers:

1. Read to children, whether from adult or children's books;
2. Tape-record stories which you and the child make up together;
3. Let the child tell you a story as you write it down;
4. Take children to preschool story hours at public libraries;
5. Sing songs which tell stories, at naptime or bedtime;
6. Play records of storytellers;
7. Give small children books and magazines which they can cut up and scribble in;
8. Help children write letters to the authors of children's books;
9. If children have imaginary playmates, ask about what the imaginary playmate is doing;
10. Let children dictate letters to relatives, playmates who are ill, legendary figures associated with family celebrations—the tooth fairy, for instance;
11. Let children dictate the stories they imagine when drawing pictures; make a "book" of the stories and pictures;
12. Help children make hand puppets and a cardboard box "theater" for plays;
13. Give children old clothing of adults, from an earlier era, if possible, and find books at the library which tell about the era from which the clothing comes;
14. Before taking trips, get library books about the region being visited and read the books to the child—at the seashore, for instance, have along a book about the ocean, seashells, terrain, and show the child the pictures and words in the book which relate to what the two of you see;
15. Children who dislike a particular food could dictate

a letter of complaint, to "Mr. Spinach Man," for instance;

16. Help children make their own greeting cards;
17. When a young child begins to recognize printed signs such as "STOP" and "McDonald's," print the signs' words on poster board at home; later, cut each individual letter into a letter-card and help the child arrange the letters into the original sign (let the child observe you writing the sign);
18. On car trips, sing "opera" with a child, with each of you "answering" the other in songs which have stories relating to the child's interests;
19. When reading favorite, familiar stories to children, stop the reading occasionally to ask the children what would happen, if, for instance, Little Red Riding Hood had decided *not* to visit her grandmother;
20. Limit television viewing until time spent reading to children at least equals the time children watch television;
21. If children watch television programs which have books relating to the TV characters, such as *Sesame Street*, get the related books from the library;
22. Help children write letters to favorite television characters;
23. Help children "produce" a children's television show of their own, with a script, cue cards;
24. Help the child make a grocery list on a large poster board, take it to the grocery store with you when you shop, and check off the items on the list as they are put in the basket, with you showing the child the proper word for the item;
25. And, again, read, read, read to children.

What to Do When Children Make Errors in Writing

It is harmful to the learning process to discipline children for what adults see as errors in writing. What is important is to discover *why* errors occur.

Small children, for instance, often like to use big words simply because they like the sounds of the words, which will, invariably, be misspelled. When this occurs, parents and teachers can: 1) help the child spell the difficult word; 2) help the child look up the word in the dictionary; 3) ignore the error while celebrating the child's delight in language; or 4) let the child dictate the word while the parent or teacher writes it for the child, exclaiming over the inventiveness of the child in selecting the word.

Often children make errors because they have no interest in the revision process. *The Magic Pencil* includes exercises designed to stimulate interest in revision.

Sometimes children make errors because they do not imagine who will read the written communication. This book also includes exercises which help children imagine an audience for their writing.

There are almost as many ways to help children learn what errors in writing are and what can be done about them as there are errors themselves. Confronting the problem or question of errors in writing can be a creative process, a part of the enjoyment of writing. *The Magic Pencil* has as one of its premises that errors in writing are *not* bad. They are a natural part of a learning process.

Exercises to Motivate Young Writers—Even Reluctant Ones

1. Give a child a number of bottles with lids (clear bottles, if possible) and ask him to imagine that inside the bottle he has found a note written by a person washed up on an isolated island. Ask him to respond to the islander. Suggest that he try to get more information from the islander about his or her circumstances; suggest that he devise various "rescue" plans to send to the islander, etc.

2. Tell the child that you've been wondering about people's habits, if, that is, most people do many of the same things day after day without noticing. Tell her that you would like to make a "study" of the habits of everyone in the family and need help. Suggest that she could help by recording on a pad of paper everyday activities, including such small things as petting the dog, brushing teeth, opening the refrigerator door, etc.

3. When reading the newspaper, mention that it leaves out a lot of news that is important to the family, such as James down the street having chicken pox and the garbage pick-up being a day late because of a holiday. Suggest that the child begin a newspaper that covers news important to people in the neighborhood. Suggest possible "stories."

4. Begin writing the dinner menu on a large piece of paper, taping it to the refrigerator. Ask the child to write a reaction beside each item on the menu.

5. Purchase a stamp pad and a set of individual rubber letters to go with the pad. Suggest that the child make his own stationery, complete with his name at the top. If an older relative needs large-print books, suggest that he write a letter to the relative, using the printing material.

6. Instead of telling a child which chores she is responsible

for, write them on a large piece of paper and tell her that she may write beside each chore how she feels about doing it. Tell her to be specific and also to write about why one chore is more pleasant to do than another. Tell her that the information may be helpful to you both when deciding on a fair distribution of chores.

7. In a paper bag, on small pieces of paper, write a number of titles for stories that relate to the child's activities: sports, toys, playmates, etc. On a rainy day or when he is bored, give the bag to him, leaving a pencil and small pad of paper in the bag. Suggest that he may want to write a story to go with one of the titles. Repeat on another rainy day.

8. If the child watches a lot of television, tell her that it would be interesting to do a "study" of what's on television—the programs and their contents, the commercials and their contents, etc. Provide the child with a large pad of paper and a pen.

9. If the child has a hero, suggest that he write a letter to the person and tell him or her why he or she is a hero and ask what it is like being a hero.

10. When the child brings home written work from school, ask her to tell you about it. As she talks, write down what she has said, including complaints. Read what you've written to the child and tell her that what she said *about* writing is a "story" too, a "story" which probably should be written by the child. Tell her that how she feels about writing at school is very important and would make an interesting book. Suggest that you and she begin writing a book *about* writing, which can include all of the child's feelings about writing.

11. Tell the child that, a long time ago, people didn't have telephones and had to send invitations and news by messenger. The next time it is convenient to replace a phone call with a written message, ask him to help you

write the message. If he enjoys this activity, use it as often as possible.

12. Study the writing your child brings home from school, noting her most frequent errors: organization, spelling, grammar, etc. When she has a writing assignment, offer to help. *Listen* to the child as she talks about the assignment and help her alleviate fears of failure by suggesting methods which will bring success. For instance, if the child fears misspelling, tell her not to worry about spelling during the writing of the first draft and remind her that many *adults* don't spell well. Say, "We'll become editors later and correct spelling then." If the child has problems organizing material, have her write the paper with several lines of space between written lines. Tell her that, after she writes the first draft, you and she will simply get some scissors, separate the sentences, and arrange them in a more logical order. Or tell the child that you can help with organization later by drawing arrows and numbering sentences. If she writes essays which seem to have none of her personality in them, ask her to think through what she would like to say and then to "tell" you the essay as you take dictation. Read the writing back to the child, asking if she wants to add anything. Putting the paper in front of her, help her reread it. Write on the draft the child's comments as she talks about the writing during the rereading. Suggest that the child now has a first draft that "sounds" like her. The key here is the listening process and approaching the child's writing problems cheerfully.

13. Give the child a diary with a lock and key.

14. If the child enjoys comics, suggest that he make his own comic strip.

NOTE: When helping a child overcome a resistance to
writing, it is important to remember that she
probably fears failure while writing. It is
especially important, then, to provide
opportunities for the child to write without fear
of censure. She needs to believe that she *can
write*.

Solving a Writing Problem

Writing is a process of discovery because the way we
communicate often demonstrates social changes. I discovered
that I did not want to write *he* when referring to "the child"
or "the young writer" because, of course, girls and boys are
equally involved in learning how to write. Yet I noticed that
writing "he or she" each time I referred to the young writer
began to sound awkward and wordy. What to do? We talked—
my editors and I—and we decided to alternate pronouns in
alternating chapters. In every other chapter I have used the
pronoun "she" when referring to the young writer and "he"
in the alternating chapters. This choice seems to make the
writing read more smoothly. The choice is one solution to a
writing problem, and there were a number of solutions to
choose from. You may want to share this writing problem
and the solution I've chosen with the young writer or writers
you're working with. Writing is a challenging process, and
the more we talk about how we make choices as writers the
better our writing may become.

Part One Learning Through Play with Language

Introduction

These exercises are designed to help young writers feel confident that writing *is* a natural way to express themselves. The focus of each exercise is on *playing* with language to make something new and exciting. Even when the exercises are designed to stimulate revision, organizational and investigational skills, or writing usually considered academic, emphasis is on playing with language. Adults helping children with these exercises will provide materials, explain exercises, and motivate children's writing by asking questions, exclaiming over children's writing, and talking with children about any writing problems they may seek adult help in solving. Adults helping children with the exercises will want to be as involved in the exercises as the *children* want them to be. The best way to help children with the exercises is to get them started, be ready to help, but don't hover.

The exercises in Part I are designed to be used in the order that they appear since the exercises are ordered to help young writers build skills by moving from one exercise to the next. The exercises may also be used out of sequence but with some loss of the building of skills.

As children "play" with language, they will also be gathering material for the exercises in Part II of the book, which will focus directly on specific writing forms and techniques. Since the exercises in Part II are more akin to writing children may do in school and to which they may have a resistance because they see such writing as "work," it is especially important for children to begin with Part I, to begin by playing with language.

Part One

Learning Through Play with Language

1. All About Me, 24
2. All About My Home, 26
3. All About My Street, 27
4. All About My Town, 28
5. A Book About Me, 30
6. Publication of a Book About Me, 32
7. The Diary of an Imaginary Person, 34
8. Drawing a Map of the Land Where the Imaginary Person Lives, 36
9. Writing Stories and Poems About the Imaginary Person, 38
10. Producing a Book from the Stories and Poems About the Imaginary Person, 40
11. Variations on Keeping a Diary of an Imaginary Person, 42
12. Stories from an Imaginary Town, 44
13. Disaster Strikes City X, 48
14. Fact-Finding Trips, 49
15. Recording Personal Histories, 50
16. Letters to and from an Imaginary Pen Pal, 51
17. Variations on the "Letters to and from an Imaginary Pen Pal" Exercise, 53
18. Changing a Story into a Play, 54
19. Changing a Poem into a Story, 57
20. Changing a Story into a Poem, 58

1 All About Me

Grades 2-9; 1st-graders will need help with writing

Supply the child with a large roll of butcher's paper for this exercise. Unroll a section as tall as the child and have him lie on it while you draw his shape. Cut off the section with the shape. Tell him that he can write all over the paper. Suggest, for instance, that he could make "hair" from a story or poem about hair, or name each toe and tell how the five toes on each foot happened to meet. You can stimulate interest in anatomy by helping the child find a book on anatomy at the library, suggesting that he write about the various internal organs, bones, muscles, etc.

Variations:

1. Using another blank shape, of an adult or child, have the young writer fill in the shape with a historical figure's story. Provide paints and crayons and books about the historical figure.
2. Suggest that the child write a story all around the shape of a person and then erase the lines drawn originally.
3. Giving the child old magazines, ask him to make a person-shaped collage of words and to glue them on top of the outlined figure.
4. Let the child ask his friends to make full-sized people on the butcher paper and to create a play involving the paper-people. Suggest the children write the dialogue on the back of each shape as they make up each character's lines.
5. Suggest that the child, using scissors, rearrange the parts of the human form, imagining, for instance, the ears as feet. Suggest the child write stories and poems on the revised form, using Scotch tape or masking tape to re-form the "person."

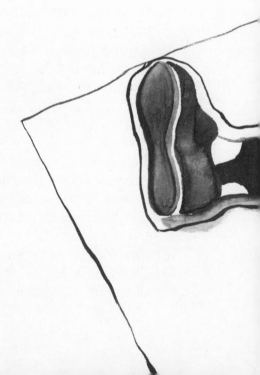

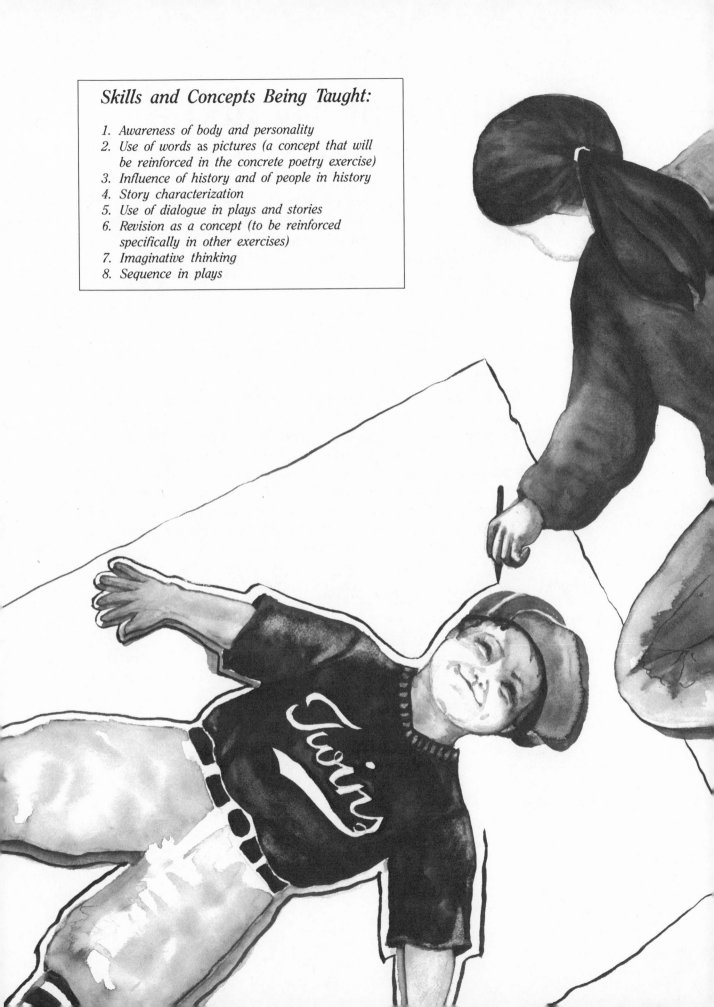

Skills and Concepts Being Taught:

1. Awareness of body and personality
2. Use of words as pictures (a concept that will be reinforced in the concrete poetry exercise)
3. Influence of history and of people in history
4. Story characterization
5. Use of dialogue in plays and stories
6. Revision as a concept (to be reinforced specifically in other exercises)
7. Imaginative thinking
8. Sequence in plays

2 All About My Home

Grades 2-9; 1st-graders will need help with writing

Give the child big sheets of paper and ask her to begin making a map of her house on a particular day, at a particular hour of the day. Tell the writer to make the drawing large and to leave room for descriptions of the rooms, the objects, the people, etc. When she has drawn the outline of the whole house or a room, suggest that she imagine that a person from another culture or place or planet has no idea of how a person such as herself lives. Ask the child to write descriptions inside the house or rooms of activities and people inside the various spaces.

At intervals, ask to see the map; ask questions about what is on the map as well as about what may yet be written. When the child is not working on the map but happens to talk about herself or her interests, mention the map. Suggest that what she's said would be an interesting addition to the map. Encourage the child to display the map on a wall in her room where, at odd times, she might add to it. Ask the child if her friends should contribute to the map, adding descriptions of visits, for instance.

Skills and Concepts Being Taught:

1. Self within a family unit
2. Close observation of people and objects within a space at a particular time
3. Writing of descriptive passages
4. Observation of and participation in an activity in writing which grows and develops over time—hence: patience, concentration
5. Concept of personality as it is displayed within a close-knit unit in a small space

3 All About My Street

Grades 2-9; 1st-graders will need help with writing

This activity is similar to the activity involving the map of the child's house. For this activity, the child should first be encouraged to begin taking notes about his street, recording on note cards what he sees, including the people who live in the neighborhood, the pets they have, their cars, gardens, television receivers; the trees in the neighborhood, the trash containers, etc. As the child takes trips to record what is in the neighborhood, encourage him to give each card a heading for identification and, when the child returns from a fact-gathering trip, suggest that he organize the notes into categories.

After this prewriting activity, give the child a very big sheet of paper and encourage him to begin drawing the map. Suggest that the map will be for a new person moving into the neighborhood who wants to know beforehand what the street he will live on is like. Suggest that the child write descriptions about each person or object he draws. Encourage him to tack the map on a wall or leave it out so that he can work on it over a period of time.

Skills and Concepts Being Taught:

1. Sense of the self in a larger world
2. Sense of interaction among people in a small area
3. Habit of observation and recording
4. Organization of material
5. Concept of people with habits and preferences which suggest personality
6. Descriptive writing
7. Descriptive writing which will have clarity to a stranger (reinforces concept of audience to be covered in later exercises)
8. Different abilities called upon by a writing activity that will take time to fulfill, in contrast to other activities in the book which can be completed more quickly

---

4 All About My Town

Grades 3-9; 1st- and 2nd-graders will need help with writing and/or organization

Talk with the child about the fact that towns are made up of dozens of streets, some with houses, some with businesses, some with parks between them, etc. Suggest that it would be interesting to make a map of her town. Ask: How many streets do you think there are? How many service stations, fire houses, libraries, ice cream stores, etc.? As she thinks about how large and complex a map of a town is, she will probably talk about making a town map as a "big job." This is the time to suggest to the child that big writing projects often need to be broken down into small segments. Suggest that it would probably be a more manageable project if the town is "divided" into sections and each section later taped together into one big map. Suggest that she may want to look at a map of the city from the library. Let the child describe to the librarian what she needs.

If possible, take the child on "fact-finding" trips, encouraging her to take notes during the trips. If the place where the child lives is too large for a practical study, have her decide how much of the city she would like to study. For younger children, a city block may be a challenging task.

Help the child divide the map into sections and encourage her to organize her notes. Suggest that the map could be made to go into a time capsule and become a record of a time in the town's history. Encourage her to decide what kinds of buildings to include and descriptions of which people; for instance, the child may want to include only stores selling food she likes to eat and people selling food who are especially friendly to children.

After the prewriting activities are underway, ask her to begin filling in sections of the map with descriptive sentences to accompany drawings. Encourage her to tape the map sections to a wall for sustained work.

Skills and Concepts Being Taught:

1. *Sense of the self in a town or city*
2. *Organizational skills*
3. *Decision-making as it relates to exclusion and inclusion of information*
4. *Close observation and note-taking for future use in writing*
5. *Descriptive writing*
6. *Descriptive writing for a reader of a future time—hence, imagination of a future time and the concept of clear writing to a stranger*

5 A Book About Me

Grades 2-9; 1st-graders will need help with writing

Ask the child to get out his map of himself. Suggest that he read what he has written about himself. Ask if anything has changed about him since he wrote and drew the map. Have the child take notes about the changes. Suggest that he write one book about himself as he *was* when the first map was drawn. Since the map was drawn over a specific time period, suggest that the child study the calendar and write down the dates during which the map was drawn. Encourage him to consider what the weather was like during the map-making period, what holidays occurred, what other special events or events in the family as a whole took place during the time period. Encourage the child to make notes as he remembers the map-making time.

Talk with the child about the differences between using first-person and third-person in a story; in other words, ask the child to consider what will be different about the book if he writes "I woke up one day and it was raining" and "He woke up one day and it was raining." Ask him if he plans to decide before writing whether to use "I" or "he." Ask whether he plans to write a book about what he can actually remember or to invent material to go with the remembered material.

Suggest to the child that when the book is finished, he could make a cover for it or xerox copies of the book's pages for friends and relatives to read. As you and the child talk about the book, ask him if a book for others to read would be different from a book which only the writer plans to read. Give the child a stack of lined paper, a set of pens or pencils, some in colors, and suggest that the child is probably ready to begin writing the book.

Note: The concept of using first-person or third-person to tell a story is not one which a child will grasp immediately. An adult can reinforce this concept by having a child select a favorite book and change the narration: if it is written in first-person, with an "I" telling the story, you or the child may talk about what would happen if every "I" were to become "he" or "she." Help the child read a few sentences revised in this way and encourage him to talk about the changes: what else will have to be changed in the story if the "I" becomes a "he" or a "she"?

Skills and Concepts Being Taught:

1. *Use of memory in writing*
2. *Concept of time in writing a narrative*
3. *Decision-making about material which is written in strict accordance with what the writer remembers and material which does not stick strictly to the facts as the writer remembers them*
4. *Use of "notes" on the map as an aid in writing narrative*
5. *Point-of-view in narration; that is, the use of the "I" or "he" or "she"*
6. *Concept that writing changes when the audience for the writing changes; that is, the concept that the writing will be different if the child's book is for anyone to read or for the child alone to read*

6 Publication of a Book About Me

Grades 2-9; 1st-graders will need help completing the project

If the young author of *All About Me* says that she has written a book which can be read by others, ask her to study the books in her library and to decide how she would like the book to look. If the child decides she wants the book to have illustrations, encourage her to read the writing she has produced and decide what pictures she should draw to go with the material. Ask the child if she would like to ask any friends to help illustrate the book. Talk with the writer about the kind of paper the book might be "printed" on. Ask her if it would be a good idea to get a book on the making of books from the library. Ask her if the book should have all the words spelled correctly and if it should have periods, commas, quotation marks, etc., in the way they are used in published books. When talking with a young writer about correcting spelling, punctuation, and grammar errors at this stage, it is important not to criticize the writer but, rather, simply to point out that published books are usually "correct" and that the writer (who is now her own publisher) will need to decide how "correct" she wants the book to be. If the child would like to produce a correct book, help her fix the writing: grammar, spelling, punctuation. If the parent is helping the child (the child may want to ask her school teacher to help with corrections), he or she may want to encourage the child to consult a dictionary and an English handbook. How much time should be spent on correcting errors and how rigorous the correcting process should be will depend on the child and her age. *Correction of errors should not dampen the young writer's interest in producing the book.* What is important is to ask the child to think about the problem of errors and to make a decision about them.

Help the writer/publisher gather the materials for making the book or books, if she wants to make multiple copies.

Depending on the age of the child and the resources of the parent or teacher, the book-making project can be simple or elaborate. For instance, an older child may become involved in producing as "correct" a book as possible, becoming interested in discovering what a copyright is, how books are bound, etc. Even if the child is not actually writing at this time, it is valuable to encourage her interest in how books are made. Later, you may want to suggest that she, having learned so much about producing a book, will want to write an essay or a story about creating a book.

When the writer has completed her first book, you may want to hold a celebration party, asking the author to sign the book. Have the writer give a reading of the book to friends and family.

Skills and Concepts Being Taught:

1. Distinction between "public" and "private" writing
2. Library research
3. Organizational skills
4. Concept that words suggest visual images for illustrations in books
5. Concept that published books usually have correct spelling, grammar and punctuation
6. Concept of an audience or readers for a book
7. Concept of using many pieces of writing written over a period of time to make a larger piece of writing

7 The Diary of an Imaginary Person

Grades 2-9; 1st-graders will need help with writing

First determine, if possible, if the child has already created an imaginary companion. If not, during quiet times you can talk with him about inventing such a companion by saying, "Let's see what we can do today—why don't we make up someone who's real to us but invisible? Should the person have a name?" By asking questions casually about the personality of the imaginary person, such as "How often does he (or she) brush his teeth?" you can help the child give fullness to the imagined person. Next, provide a book with blank pages or a lined note pad and suggest that he begin letting the imaginary person "write" about what happens to him, her or "it" every day. Occasionally ask the child what the imaginary character did "today"; at other times, after or before, for instance, a visit to the dentist ask him if the imaginary person (who will by now have a name) has to visit the dentist, or attend school, take piano lessons, etc. When the young writer stops working on the diary, refrain from prodding but simply ask if the imaginary person is on vacation or sick with the flu. (Do not be surprised if the child says that the imaginary person has died, a common comment for children between four and seven. Soon the child will bring the imaginary person back to life.) Ask if the child wants to read the diary to you; you may also want to ask if the imaginary person plans to publish the diary or if it's too private.

Skills and Concepts Being Taught:

1. *Imaginative thinking*
2. *Importance of imagination*
3. *Characterization; detail as an aspect of characterization*
4. *Sustained writing, its possibilities*
5. *Writing in sequence*
6. *Diary publication as a possibility*
7. *Distinction between "private" and "public" writing*

35

8 Drawing a Map of the Land Where the Imaginary Person Lives

Grades 2-9; 1st-graders may need adult help

After providing her with large sheets of paper, ask the young writer to reread the imaginary person's diary and make a list of what the imaginary person (I.P.) has done and the places he or she or "it" has been. If she shares the list with you, you may want to ask such questions as "Oh, he (or she or 'it') doesn't have any pets?" or "Where do the grandparents live?" or "Is she (or he or 'it') old enough to drive?" When the child has made her list, suggest that she make a picture *and* word map of the imaginary person's town. Suggest that the child:

a) draw the buildings first;

b) with numbers, indicate what the imaginary person does each day, numbering the house where he, she, or "it" wakes up as (1) and the school house as (2) etc.;

c) suggest that the child then connect the numbers with words which describe a busy day in the life of the imaginary person.

Skills and Concepts Being Taught:

1. *Using a piece of writing to produce something else*
2. *Sequencing of events*
3. *Methods of expanding imaginative writing*
4. *Techniques of writing short, expository sentences for the purpose of clarifying a sequence of activities*

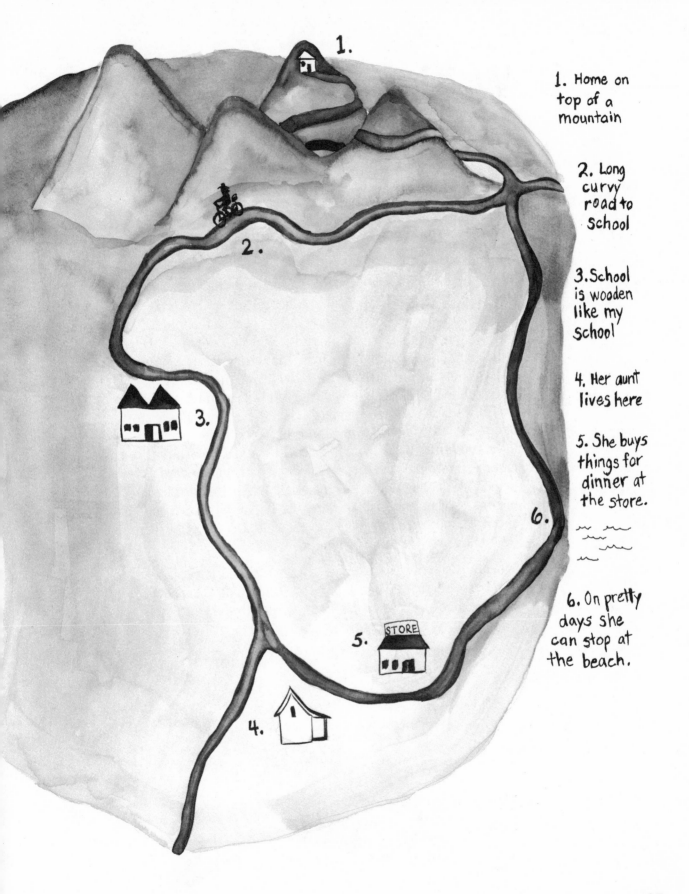

1. Home on top of a mountain

2. Long curvy road to school

3. School is wooden like my school

4. Her aunt lives here

5. She buys things for dinner at the store.

6. On pretty days she can stop at the beach.

9 Writing Stories and Poems About the Imaginary Person

Grades 2-9; 1st-graders will need help with writing

Since the young writer now has a diary of the I.P.'s activities and a map of the I.P.'s town, he has plenty of material for poems and stories. In later exercises, specific techniques used in poetry writing and story writing will be developed. Here it will be important simply to help the writer learn to separate a small amount of possible material from the wealth of material the writer has created in the diary and map exercises. Suggest, for instance, that the child write a story about the I.P.'s last day of school before summer vacation or a poem about the fish in the dentist's office or about the ice cream stand. You will need to look at his map in order to help him narrow down the material. When the stories and poems are finished, ask the child if he would like to publish the imaginary person's book, become, that is, a publisher, explaining what a publisher does, briefly.

Provide the writer with many sheets of lined paper and a number of pens, all one color this time. Tell the child not to worry about making errors as he writes.

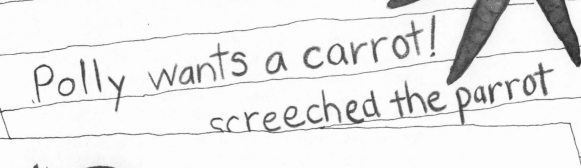

Polly wants a carrot! screeched the parrot

She lives in Australia and her best friend is a big old kangaroo.

10 Producing a Book from the Stories and Poems About the Imaginary Person

Grades 2-9; 1st-graders will need assistance

Give the writer books of poems, stories, and books containing both stories and poems, some with illustrations, some without. If possible, find a book which is an anthology, containing poems and stories by a variety of writers whose writing has been chosen for inclusion in the book by an editor. Ask the child how she imagines that an editor decides what stories and poems to include. Suggest that she may want to reread all of the stories about the imaginary person and select only a few to include in the book. If any of the child's poems and stories are written in first-person, with an "I" telling the story, ask the writer if she wants to pretend that the imaginary person actually wrote the poem or story. Ask her if her friends would like to "meet" the imaginary person and write about him, her, or "it." Ask if the child's friends would like to write poems and stories about imaginary people *they* know and include them in the book.

Tell the writer that she is about to become an editor and publisher; as in the exercise A Book About Me (pages 30-31), help the child make a decision about errors: to correct or not. If the child chooses not to correct errors, tell her that the book may be more difficult for others to read and ask if she plans to have anyone else read the book. If she wants to correct errors, provide a dictionary and an English handbook and answer the child's questions about spelling, etc.

As in the exercise on pages 32-33, the book production may be simple or elaborate. Let the writer's interest determine how complicated the project will be. Provide materials, including resource material about book production if she shows interest in the process.

When the book is complete, look at it with the writer, exclaiming over each selection. Ask her what material she decided to leave out. As she explains, you may suggest that she show you the omitted material and tell you why she decided to leave it out.

Ask the child if she would like to have a party to celebrate the "publication" of the book. Since the Imaginary Person will not be able to attend his or her own publication party, you may suggest that the child write a telegram from the I.P. explaining why he or she couldn't attend the party. Alternately, to stimulate imagination, you may suggest that the child create a life-sized puppet or "dummy" of the I.P. so that he or she can attend the party.

Skills and Concepts Being Taught:

1. Book editing as a process of selection
2. Concept of what makes an anthology of creative work
3. Concept that written material published for an audience will be more easily understood if "errors" are corrected
4. Concept that writing is a form of communication which may stimulate others to want to communicate through writing

11 Variations on Keeping a Diary of an Imaginary Person

Grades 3-9; 1st- and 2nd-graders will need help with writing

The material a child studies at school can become material for diary exercises. You may suggest:

1. diaries "by" historical figures;

2. diaries "by" the authors of books he reads at school: ask him to imagine who has written the book, how the writer might have been thinking as he or she wrote the book, what the author may have had to research in the library in order to write the book. If there is dialogue in the books the child reads at school, ask him how he thinks the writer "knows" what the characters said. Suggest that the child pretend he is the writer of the book and is keeping a diary about his work on it;

3. diaries "by" parents, friends, teachers: ask the child if he ever imagines what others might write in their diaries and suggest that he make several diaries "for" a friend, parent, teacher.

Skills and Concepts Being Taught:

1. *Diaries by historical figures:*
   a. *Books of facts can become material for imaginative writing*
   b. *Academic writing and imaginative writing are not wholly separate types of writing*
   c. *Historical figures have personal lives and thoughts*
2. *Diaries "by" the authors of books the child reads at school:*
   a. *Professional writers make decisions about writing problems just as the child-writer does and confront similar writers' problems*
   b. *Dialogue of historical figures, for instance, may be invented by the professional writer or may be taken from historical documents; dialogue in writing is a skill which can be considered and studied*
   c. *Recognizing that books by professional writers are written in small sections just as the child writer produces a book*
   d. *Concept that sometimes professional writers must do library research in order to write a book*
3. *Diaries "by" parents, friends, etc.*
   a. *Imagining others' private thoughts and imagining others as living day-to-day lives which include duties and roles distinct from those the child may know the person in*
   b. *Writing as a method of gaining perspective about others: using writing as means of broadening the imagination*

Note: This exercise also provides the child with a means of expressing anger and frustration in an acceptable form, which teaches the concept that writing is a form of expression which can be a substitute for physically acting out some emotions.

12 Stories from an Imaginary Town

Grades 2-9; 1st-graders will need assistance

This exercise is designed to work well with one child or a group of children, who can stimulate each other's interest. Provide large sheets of paper or long sections of paper from a roll. Begin the activity by asking the children: "If you were going to build a town where no town has existed before, where would you build it, what would you have in it, what would you build first, who would come to live in the town, who would arrive first?" and so on. Ask the group if they would choose to build a modern town, a futuristic town, or one from the past. When the group has imagined a number of the aspects of the town, ask that they begin "building" the town, working together, on the sheet of paper. Encourage the use of various materials by providing, for instance, glue and sticks, colored pencils and pens; suggest that the children may want to collect additional building materials.

When the group appears to have completed the town, suggest that they now consider what type of government the town will have, who will "run" the government, how sanitation, electricity (if any), water, heat, etc., will be provided. Ask them to consider what work the town's citizens will do, what will motivate the people to move to the town, etc. Ask if there will be a newspaper in the town, ask about forms of entertainment, etc.

Note: The following are suggested activities, which can be modified in accordance to the age or ages of the children involved.

Writing activities: For one child or a group

1. Write a history of the town's development for a group of construction engineers who are interested in learning how a new town is made.
2. Begin a newspaper for the town, with editorials, comic

strips, letters to the editor, news articles, sports pages, interviews, "profiles" of town citizens, reports of school activities, advice columns, weather reports, financial news, etc. (1st- and 2nd-graders will benefit from being given suggestions and limited guidance.)

3. Write a set of documents about governance in the town; encourage older children to research the project before beginning writing. 1st- and 2nd-graders may simply want to make up "Rules."

4. Write letters to out-of-town businesses who may respond to an invitation to relocate in the new town.

5. Write letters "from" town dwellers to friends and relatives who have not yet visited the new town.

6. Plan, in writing, a new educational system, including types of classes, codes of dress, length of school day and year. Begin a school newspaper.

7. Make a "time capsule" to be buried somewhere in town and fill the capsule with objects and written documents which explain them.

8. Write a "report," imagining that the first year of the town's life has passed and that the city fathers are going to read the report in order to plan for future growth and development.

9. Organize in writing, an art center for the town, if one has not been built. If the town has no artists, write letters or brochures which will entice artists to move to or visit the town. When the artists "arrive," write advertising copy, programs, posters, etc., to draw the audience.

10. Imagining that the town is five years old, write a history and assessment of the town, including its good aspects as well as those which need improvement.

11. For the fifth-year town celebration, produce a book containing stories and poems "by" citizens of the town. Write a play about the development and growth of the town. Write the words to a town anthem or song.

Skills and Concepts Being Taught:

In this exercise, the word "story" in the title of the exercise is used in its broadest sense, to suggest that a town has a story which is "told" in many ways. Documents have stories behind them, as do letters to the editor, articles on sporting events, etc.

This exercise focuses mainly on a writer's flexibility with form and language. While all the material will be invented, imagined, some of the written work will be expository prose, some fiction, some poetry, some bits of writing in advertisements, signs, etc. The challenge to the young writer is to decide what type of writing is appropriate to a given assignment, for a particular audience.

This exercise also stimulates long-term concentration and the building of imagination as ideas seed new ideas.

The various exercises also focus on the concept of "voice" in writing; that is, writers in grades 3-9 will write in different styles, some formal and others informal, when doing various writing assignments. Later writing exercises will reinforce the concept of "voice" in specific activities designed to help young writers become aware of "voice" as an aspect of writing.

Some of the writing exercises encourage writers to do library research.

13 Disaster Strikes City X

Grades 2-9; 1st-graders will need assistance

This exercise focuses on contrast—the town which the child or children have built will now, like a child's sand castle at the beach, meet with some disaster. Tell the children to imagine that the town has been nearly destroyed by something and help the writer or writers decide what has destroyed the town. Then ask them to make lists: of the town's citizens, its buildings, its organizations, etc. When the lists are made, provide a large paper bag and ask the writers to make up titles of pieces of writing which will, in various ways, document the town's destruction. Help with suggestions which vary widely, such as: a letter from the mayor to the President of the United States asking for relief assistance; "How My Dog Bowser Died"; "A Fishy Story"; "Local Cheerleaders Stranded at Jason's Cove"; "Money Found Floating in Stream Twenty Miles Beyond City X," etc.

When the writers have written titles for various types of stories on note paper, have them put the titles in the paper bag, shake the bag, and let each writer "draw" a title and write an appropriate story.

When the stories and essays and news stories have been written, suggest that the child or children decide if they would like to make their writing public by "publishing" the writing in some form. Help the writers decide how to publish the material and what they want to do about technical errors in the writing (see pages 32-33).

Skills and Concepts Being Taught:

1. *Use of writing to stimulate new writing*
2. *Imagination*
3. *"Voice" in writing (different titles will suggest to the writers that it is appropriate to consider what style of writing the title calls for)*
4. *Movement between different types of writing*
5. *Writing for an audience*
6. *Decision-making about errors in writing*

14 Fact-Finding Trips

Grades 2-9; 1st-graders will need assistance

Provide the child with a number of small notebooks on which you or she has written: Grocery Store, Dry Cleaners, School, Library, Post Office, Restaurants, Gas Stations, etc. Try to provide a notebook for each place the child frequents. Tell her that detail in writing is what provides "spice" or suggest that the writer imagine that she is a spy or will write a report. If possible, hang the small notebooks near the door from which she normally exits the home to encourage her to take a notebook or notebooks with her on trips. Suggest that she try to notice as much about a place as possible and to write the details and facts in the notebooks.

Suggest that the writer notice changes in places which occur at different times of the day, in different seasons.

Skills and Concepts Being Taught:

1. *Detail as an aid to writing*
2. *Attention to detail*
3. *Gathering of material for future writing projects*
4. *Sustained writing project*

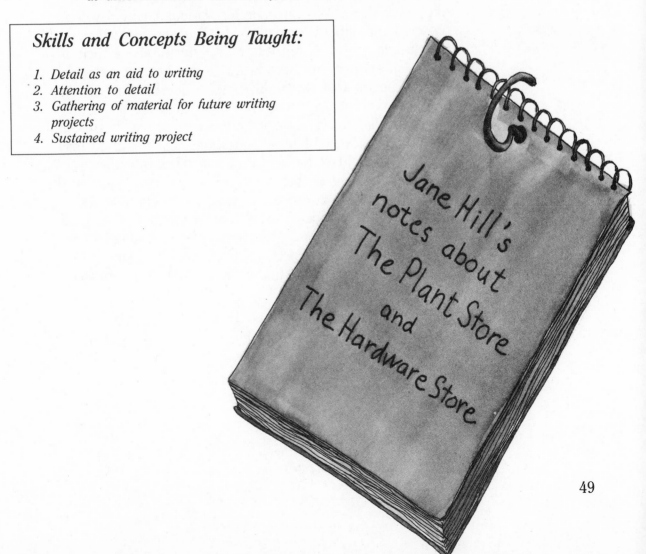

Jane Hill's notes about The Plant Store and The Hardware Store

15 Recording Personal Histories

Grades 3-9; 1st- and 2nd-graders may find the exercise overly difficult

Since children find distant eras and cultures fascinating, it helps to begin this activity by providing young writers with books, either fiction or nonfiction, about people who have lived in earlier times. You may want to ask the child to tell you what he has learned about the various eras: places, customs, traditions.

Provide the young writer with a notebook and pencil and suggest that he might like to interview older family members, neighbors, teachers, friends about what life was like "back then." You can mention various changes you've observed throughout your own life. You may also suggest that people can often tell interesting stories about their lives which others may not have heard simply because no one has asked. Suggest that the child think of questions he would like to ask an older person and write them down. As the writer begins interviewing, if he wants to share the material with you, it is helpful to ask questions that the child may not have thought of about the person he is interviewing. You may want to suggest that he focus on a single aspect of the person's life, such as service in a war, how clothing was styled, methods of food storage and preparation, how boys and girls socialized, etc. After the writer is involved in the interviewing/writing project, ask him what he plans to do with the material, suggesting a book made of a series of transcribed interviews.

> ## Skills and Concepts Being Taught:
>
> 1. *Interest in history*
> 2. *Preparation for a writing project*
> 3. *Organization*
> 4. *Research techniques apart from research in printed material*
> 5. *Question of audience for written material*
> 6. *Connection to adults and their personal histories*

16 Letters to and from an Imaginary Pen Pal

Grades 2-9; 1st-graders may need help with writing

This exercise is designed to help a young writer make use both of the writing done and the methods of gathering information used in several previous exercises.

1. Ask the child to read the writing she did for exercises 1-6.

2. Ask her to tell you or to list the categories of information contained in the writing from exercises 1-6: school, home, relatives, hobbies, food, pets, likes and dislikes, etc.

3. Ask her to read again the diary of an Imaginary Person she wrote for Exercise 7 and to list the categories of information that the Imaginary Person revealed in the diary.

4. Ask the child to think about what she doesn't yet know about the Imaginary Person. Suggest that she list what she doesn't know but would like to know.

5. Providing the writer with lined stationery, envelopes, and stamps, suggest that she begin a correspondence with the Imaginary Person. Tell her that, as she writes her own letters and "answers" the return letters from the Imaginary Person, she may want to discover how many different things about the Imaginary Person she can find out.

6. Show the writer different types of letters—personal and business—and ask her which style of letter writing would be most appropriate for the imagined person.

Skills and Concepts Being Taught:

1. Research
2. Organization of materials for future writing project
3. Writing which has a specific goal
4. Imagination
5. Expository writing
6. Form of letters
7. Rewards of a writing project which extends over time

52

17 Variations on the "Letters to and from an Imaginary Pen Pal" Exercise

1. Using the "Variations on Keeping a Diary of an Imaginary Friend" material on pages 42-43 and any writing which the young writer has written for the variations, suggest that the writer may want to write letters to and "from" a historical figure.

2. Suggest that you and the writer substitute letter writing for several other forms of communication. For instance, you may suggest that, instead of your telling him what his weekly chores are, you will now write letters about doing the chores and that he can answer the letters with letters of his own in which he expresses his feelings about each chore.

3. Suggest that the child choose a favorite friend or relative to correspond with and encourage him to share in the letters news of very small or insignificant events such as setting the table, washing the blackboard at school, buying stamps at the post office, etc.

4. Suggest that the writer write letters to authors of favorite books, asking the authors what they will write about in their next book. Suggest that the child "answer" these letters.

5. Some children's authors answer letters from children. If the child would like to see if one of his favorite authors will answer his letter, talk with him about what he would most like to ask the author and what he would most like to say to the author about a favorite book. Ask the child to talk with his school or public librarian about finding the author's address or the address of the author's publisher.

18 Changing a Story into a Play

Grades 3-9; modifications required for younger children follow the description of the activity

Help the young writer find a book which she especially likes and one which can be written in. Give her two transparent markers of distinctly different colors. Tell her that sentences which are spoken by characters will have quotation marks around them, as in "I want to write a play." Tell the writer that this is the *dialogue* in the story and that the rest of the writing in the story is the *narration*. Suggest that she underline all of the dialogue with one color of marker and all of the narration with another colored marker. An alternative method of separating dialogue from narration is to have the writer first number each sentence, then cut the sentences into sections, separating dialogue from narration and then pasting the story parts on poster board, staggering the sections:

1. Jack was Timmy's new neighbor. Jack watched Timmy as Timmy stood by the moving van.

              2. "Mom,"

2. said Jack,

              2. "I'm going to meet the new boy next door, ok?"

3. Jack ran across the yard.

When the writer understands the difference between dialogue and narration, tell her that, in plays, what we hear spoken is dialogue and narration becomes *stage directions,* which only the actors and the director read to know how to perform the dialogue.

If possible, have the writer borrow a play from the library so that she can see how dialogue and stage directions are put on a page. Give her a set of file cards and suggest that she write the story dialogue on cards. Then suggest that the writer change the story narration into directions about what each character does: Jack runs across stage, from left to right. Suggest that she may be helped by drawing a number of pictures of a stage and writing on file cards what is on the stage, when the *scenery* changes, what *sound effects* will need to be in the play, etc. Suggest that the writer may want to invent new dialogue for the characters and even change the order of events in the story—maybe the story happens in the morning and the writer would prefer to have it happen in the middle of the night. When she has the material from the story and her own invented material on separate file cards, some with dialogue and some with stage directions and descriptions, suggest that the writer spread the cards out on the floor so that she can look at them all, adding any she needs to begin writing a play. Suggest that she may want to shuffle the cards around to see if a brand-new story could be made from the cards.

When the writer has decided on the play she wants to put on paper, suggest that she copy the cards on the paper in such a way that a stranger could understand from reading what would happen on stage.

Changing a Story into a Play—Variations for Young Children

1. When reading to young children, read what characters say in a voice different from that used when reading narration. Exaggerate the voices of characters by "becoming" the Big Bad Wolf or Little Red Riding Hood.

2. When a child becomes familiar with the story and knows what the characters say, suggest that she say the characters' words while you read only the narration.

3. Provide sound effects, by voice and by finding household objects which produce sounds appropriate to the story. A child can help find objects which could be used for sound effects.

4. Read stories which you and the child can act out by using household objects as props. Ask other family members and her friends to help.

5. Help the child make paper-bag or sock puppets of the story characters, which she can use as you read the story.

6. Before reading a familiar story, ask the child to tell *you* the story. Occasionally ask her to tell the story but to stop when she comes to a part during which a character talks—*you* will say the dialogue.

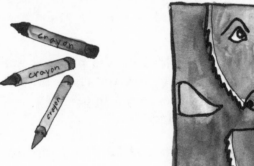

Lunch - sack puppets

1. Draw the character's features on construction paper. What is most important to your character? Eyes, ears, a hat, teeth, a funny nose, big eyebrows, a silly smile?

2. Cut them out.

3. Glue them to your sack.

← Example: A Big Bad Wolf !

19 Changing a Poem into a Story

Grades 2-9; 1st-graders will need help with writing

Tell the writer that many poems have hidden stories in them. Suggest that he play the game "Can you find the story?" by reading a poem and asking: 1) who is in the poem? 2) where does the person "live" during the poem: one place, several places? 3) what does the person in the poem do? 4) why does the person or thing in the poem do whatever it is he or she or it does? 5) what happens to the "character" in the poem? 6) can the person who wrote the poem be a character in the poem?

Suggest that the writer write a story which tells in *narration* and *dialogue* the story of the poem.

Note: For this exercise, it is most helpful if the poems the writer uses are *not* narrative, story-telling poems such as "Paul Revere's Ride." Help the writer find poems in which the story is hidden to some degree.

Skills and Concepts Being Taught:

1. *Using one piece of writing to produce another*
2. *Difference between the story form and the poetry form*
3. *Revision, rearrrangement of language*
4. *Concept of poetry as story*
5. *Concept of compression in poetry; that is, the concept that poetry often suggests material without directly presenting it*
6. *Concept of character in poetry and, hence, a similarity between poetry and stories*
7. *Concept that poetry can have the writer as a character in the "story" of the poem*
8. *Visualization of a "picture" suggested by few words in a poem, which aids the writer in the practice of close reading of poetry*

20 Changing a Story into a Poem

Grades 2-9; 1st-graders may need help with writing

Give the writer a book of stories and a book of poems and ask her to tell you what looks different about stories and poems. (Try to find a poetry book that contains poems in a large variety of shapes.)

Suggest that the writer change a story into a poem by shaping it like a poem, adding new words or leaving words out. When she has shaped a story into lines of poetry, suggest that she might enjoy having the poem change shape too. Ask her to see how many different ways she can shape the words into new poems. Ask the writer if words can become "pictures" on a page. Provide different colors of pens and suggest that she may want to color the words.

Skills and Concepts Being Taught:

1. *Using one piece of writing to produce another piece of writing*
2. *Revision*
3. *Poetry form as different from story form*
4. *Concept of words as pictures in poetry*

58

Ploffskin, Pluffskin, Pelican jee,
We think no Birds so happy as we!
Plumpskin, Ploshkin, Pelican jill,
We think so then, and we thought so still!

Yes, they came; and among the rest,
The King of the Cranes all grandly dressed
Such a lovely tail! Its feathers float
Between the ends of his blue dress-coat;
With pea-green trousers all so neat,
And a delicate frill to hide his feet,
(For though no one speaks of it, every one knows
He has got no webs between his toes!)

—from *The Pelican Chorus*
Edward Lear

59

Part Two   A Focus on Skills

Introduction

In Part I young writers focused on exploring themselves as writers through projects which focused primarily on content and only secondarily on technique and specific writing skills. The exercises in Part II will focus on helping them develop specific skills in many forms of writing, and a number of the exercises will provide opportunities for revision and editing. As in Part I the exercises will help the young writer move freely between types of writing we often term "creative" and "academic." The exercises may at first glance appear to be arbitrarily ordered so that a writer following the sequence will move from writing a research report to writing a poem. Actually, the order reflects the natural process of moving back and forth between creative and academic writing activities. The young writer will not be asked, then, to do only writing normally considered academic for a long period of time as if his or her creative writing were not equally important. Rather, a sequence of skills is available within exercises calling for a variety of types of writing. Report writing calls for creative thinking, and an exercise about story writing, for instance, involves organizational skills.

Part II exercises call for more adult cooperation with the writer than the exercises in Part I did. While all of the exercises encourage young writers to enjoy manipulating language for expression, involvement with the Part II exercises teaches more sophisticated skills. Adults helping childen work with these exercises should take care to maintain a "fun" environment even as the exercises become more complex. Adults will want to guide and suggest, not scold young writers about errors. A good teacher of writing is a good listener and a good conversationalist.

Parents who have used Part I will be able to adapt any of the exercises in Part II to a level appropriate to their young writer or writers. For that reason, grade levels are not specified for these exercises. (Exercise 20 is an exception—the sophistication about vocabulary it requires would make it difficult for first- and second-graders). Adults supervising work in Part II should remain flexible and sensitive to the level at which their young writer(s) feel(s) challenged and comfortable.

Part Two

A Focus on Skills

1. Making Writing Visual: The Simile, 64
   a. A Poem Using Similes, 64
   b. Revising Written Work: Adding Similes, 65
   c. The Silly-Simile Game, 67
   d. Similes to Express Strong Feelings, 68
2. Turning the Simile into a Metaphor, 70
3. Stories That Begin with Metaphors, 72
4. Metaphor as Disguise, 73
5. Developing Contemplation in a Young Writer, 74
6. Revision After Contemplation, 77
7. Metaphorical Writing Following a Trip, 78
8. What Is Poetry?, 80
9. A Book About Poetry, 81
10. Helping Young Writers Correct Errors, 83
11. Learning to Organize from Activity, 86
12. From Letters to Essays, 88
13. The Writer Becomes an Editor, 90
14. Methods of Research, 92
15. Making Stories More Complete, 94
16. Research by Interviewing, 96
17. Writing an Essay from an Interview, 98
18. The Reader or Audience for Writing, 100
19. Concrete Poetry, 101
20. Vocabulary-Building Simile Poem Using Synonyms, 102
21. Words Reveal How We Feel, 104
22. Giving a Story's Main Character Personality, 105
23. Writing Stimulated by Writing and Combined with Revision, 108
24. What Happens When I Write?, 109
25. Talking to the Author, 111
26. Brainstorming, 112

1 Making Writing Visual: The Simile

In the following exercises, the writer will focus on visual writing by using similes. A *simile* likens one thing to another by use of the words *like* or *as*. These are visual comparisons, as in "Night is like the black mane of a horse covering the sun" or "a runner puffing like a steam engine" or "a coat as white as thistledown." In everyday speech, we use comparisons frequently: "nervous as a kitten" or "so tired I could drop like a dog."

a. A Poem Using Similes

Prewriting exercise: Talk with the writer about things which are hard to describe, such as time passing, the way a person walks, hoping for something, how a color makes a person feel. Tell him that it often helps to describe something by saying it is like something else. Ask him to wiggle his toes and compare the wiggling to something else that wiggles. Ask the writer to look at the color of his eyes in a mirror and to compare his eyes to something else that color. Ask him to find something soft and tell you how soft the object is by comparing it to something else. He will quickly understand the use of similes in speech. Many of those similes will, however, be trite because he hears similes frequently; "as busy as a bee" and "as sticky as molasses" are common similes which, if used in writing, would not help a reader "see" something newly. What the writer will need to do in order to make fresh similes is to use his own vision and feelings. Give him, then, a list of colors: purple, red, white, and black. Ask him to close his eyes and to think of nothing but the color white. Ask him to think about how white objects make him feel. Is "white" soft, hard, heavy, light, smooth, rough?

Writing activity: When the writer opens his eyes, ask him to put the title "What White Is Like" on a piece of paper and to write a poem comparing "white" to other things. Try the same exercise for other colors. Tell the writer he has been using *similes*. Ask him to read his simile poems to you.

Reinforcement activities:
1. When reading with the writer, ask him to point out any similes he notices.
2. Consciously insert similes into requests you make of the writer. Say such things as "Quick as a bird, wash your face" or "Chug like a locomotive up the stairs" or "Sleep as soundly as a bear in winter."

Skills and Concepts Being Taught:

1. *A method of making writing visual*
2. *Thinking comparatively*
3. *Selecting words to clarify other words*
4. *Concentration on individual words to make writing specific*
5. *Concept that a writer's feelings, sensations, and experiences are an aid in creating interesting sentences*

---

b. Revising Written Work: Adding Similes

Prewriting exercise: Ask the young writer to look through her essays in the "All About My Town" folder or to look at the writing on the map of her own town. Ask her to choose a small section of the town to talk about with you. Tell the child that you want to imagine that a stranger will be learning about that particular part of the town and will need to be able to "see" it in his or her mind, to imagine it. Say that one of the best ways to make something visual is to compare it to something else. Talk with her about comparing a section of sidewalk to, for instance, a rectangular cake without frosting. Ask what the church spire is like, etc. If the child has previously written an essay about the town, suggest that she read it and make marks on it where a comparison of one thing in the essay could be made if something were added or inserted. If she hasn't already written an essay about the town, ask her to tell you about a section of it, comparing the way something looks to something not on the map.

Writing activity: If the writer is working with previously written material, ask her to write a comparison for one thing in the writing on a small piece of paper. For instance, if the essay contains the word *sidewalk*, the child might write on the scrap of paper: *like a gray ribbon*. When a number of words have been supplemented with similes, have the child place the scraps of paper with similes on them just above the words they go with and then have her read the new piece of writing. As you listen, say such things as, "Yes! I can *see* it's like a gray ribbon." Suggest that she write out the "new" essay on a clean piece of paper, adding any additional similes she may think of.

If the writer hasn't yet written an essay about a part of her town, suggest that she write a description to a stranger, using comparisons to objects the stranger might know if he or she lived anywhere. As the child writes, she may want your participation in thinking of comparisons. It will help her to visualize the objects if she makes quick sketches of them. You may help with comments such as "Well, a bridge from a distance looks as if it's floating in the air—what else floats in the air?"

When the young writer makes a comparison, it is important to exclaim over it, even if the comparison is farfetched and doesn't truly seem appropriate to an adult. A bridge *may* seem to squat like a duck to a child's way of seeing.

Reinforcement activity: Since this writing activity works with both similes and revision, it is helpful, when reading with a child, to notice the similes in the text and to wonder aloud if the writer thought of the comparison in the first draft or later added it to make the writing more visual. You may want to encourage the child to identify places in the text where a comparison might have made the writing more visual and interesting.

c. The Silly-Simile Game

Theory: Young writers can learn to refine comparisons—that is, use comparisons which liken two things in such a way as to have a reader genuinely "see" something newly—by using comparisons which are silly and outlandish. Their laughing about silly comparisons will help them want *not* to make silly comparisons in their writing, unless the intention is to write comedy. This game, then, is designed to allow writers to play with language while also refining their understanding of similes.

The game: You, the young writer, and any other children available (the more the merrier) need a stack of three-inch by five-inch file cards or strips of paper. A colorful set of magic markers adds to the enjoyment, and color can also suggest language. First, have the group write names of things, in large letters, each on a separate card, including proper names. Next, write a number of verbs—action verbs such as *ran, skipped, stirred, whipped, punched,* etc. Finally, write on the cards a number of half-similes, each beginning with the words *like* or *as*: like a whale spouting; like a butterfly; like a ball spinning in the sky; etc.

Have each person in the group draw a card from the "noun" stack and place it on the table or floor. Then have each player draw a card from the "verb" stack and place it, face down, on the table beside the "noun" card. Finally, have each player draw a "simile" card and place it, face down, by the "verb" card. Then have all the players at once turn their cards to discover whose sentence is the silliest. Suggest that the players exchange cards with one another to make a new "silly simile." Then ask if anyone can come up with a simile which isn't "silly." Play the game several more times until each player has three or four sentences. Suggest that a "silly story" might be made of all of the sentences, by arrangement and rearrangement. When the group has decided on a story, ask one of the players if he or she would like to write it down to keep. Suggest that, later, a book might be made of the "silly-simile stories."

Skills and Concepts Being Taught:

1. Difference between similes which can easily be understood by the reader and similes which a reader would find "silly"
2. Identification of nouns
3. Writing as an extension of play with words

---

d. Similes to Express Strong Feelings

Introduction: Young writers need to be encouraged to express in writing the range of their feelings in order to understand that feelings are as important as facts and can be put into writing in many ways. The following exercise will focus on using similes to express strong likes and dislikes the young writer may have.

Prewriting exercise: Ask the writer to make two lists, one titled "Things I Like" and the other "Things I Don't Like." When both lists have a number of items on them, ask the writer to pick one thing he especially likes or dislikes. After he makes a choice, ask him to think about what it's like to be involved with the thing or person or activity.

Writing activity: Ask the writer to write a poem, story, or essay about what he has chosen to describe and to write about it by comparing it to something else or to many things. Ask him to see how many of his feelings he can have come out in comparisons.

Note: The writer may exaggerate or choose to write strongly about something in a way which reveals feelings he may have kept hidden previously. It is important for the adult helping the writer not to express alarm or to censure the child's writing.

Skills and Concepts Being Taught:

1. Concept that how a writer feels is important in writing
2. Use of similes to express feelings
3. Using notes and lists as a preparation for writing in form

Spinach
The green goo
slides down
your throat
like slimy
worms

2 Turning the Simile into a Metaphor

Introduction: A metaphor is similar to a simile since it, too, is a type of comparison, except that the words *like* and *as* are dropped. One thing, then, is actually *called* another thing or assumes qualities of another thing. When we say "The wind *bites*," the wind has taken on the properties of an animal, even though the animal is not named. When we say that someone is "bubbling over," we suggest a boiling pan of water or a brook. When we say "The night sleeps under a cover of moonlight," we suggest a person sleeping under a summer-weight blanket, perhaps. This is *metaphorical language*.

Prewriting exercise: Have the writer get out her "simile" cards made for the "Silly-Simile Game" and separate the ones beginning with *like* or *as* from the stack. Give her scissors and masking tape and ask her to cut the words *like* and *as* apart from the card. Then have her tape those words onto the card by applying masking tape to the back so that *like* and *as* will fold back and be hidden. Then ask her to separate the nouns from the stack. Ask her to make a set of partial sentences using nouns first and then, beside each noun, a simile card with the words *like* or *as* folded back. Ask the child to move the cards around until she creates a phrase she likes. (You might see, then, such phrases as: *Lion* (the noun) *a sailboat* (the simile with *like* folded back); *cars* (the noun) *ants on a mound*.

Writing exercise: Ask the writer to imagine, for instance, the lion *as* a sailboat and to complete the sentence by using a verb associated with a sailboat. If the child writes, for example, "A lion, a sailboat in the grass, glides to the tree," encourage her to "play" with the metaphors: "A lion sails in the grass" (the lion becomes a sailboat with the verb *sails*) or "Sailing through the grass, the lion docks under a canopy of leaves" (*sailing* and *docks* suggesting the lion as sailboat and *canopy* suggesting the tree).

If you give the writer several suggestions, she will not only quickly grasp what a metaphor is but also begin actively to participate in revision that makes writing more vivid.

Reinforcement activities:

1. Ask the writer to participate with you in making a list of metaphorical phrases for use in future poems. Write on an index card: "The wind tiptoes through the trees." Getting out a new card, ask the writer to think of a phrase.
2. When reading to a child or talking with a young writer about what she is reading, point out metaphorical language or ask her if she has found any metaphors. Again, wonder out loud if the writer thought of the metaphors during the composing of the first draft or during later drafts.

Skills and Concepts Being Taught:

1. *Difference between similes and metaphors*
2. *Identification of and focus on verbs*
3. *Revision of writing to make sentences more visual*
4. *Concept that a metaphor can help a writer use more exact and visual verbs*

3 Stories That Begin with Metaphors

Introduction: This exercise will encourage a young writer in using metaphorical language as a way of thinking. It will also encourage him to build on previously written work in order to demonstrate how thinking about one piece of writing can become preparation for another.

Prewriting exercise: Ask the writer to get out his "Disaster Strikes City X" folder, which should have in it news stories, essays, and stories. Ask him to read to you a number of the "disasters." As he reads, write titles for stories on separate cards, turning the people or objects into something else. For instance, if a flood hit City X and you discover from listening to one of the child's news stories that twenty cows drowned in the flood, write as a title something like: "The Day the Cows Became a Fleet of Ships." If a bomb hit City X, write a title such as "The Day the Flowers Packed Up Their Petals and Went Home." If the children at the school went through a fire drill, you might write: "The Day Two Hundred Ducklings Left School for an Hour." Tell the writer that you've made a story game from the disasters. Put the story titles in a paper bag and let him choose one to write a story about, combining what he can learn from the title with information in the news stories, essays, and previously written stories.

Skills and Concepts Being Taught:

1. *Building on previously written work to produce new writing*
2. *Using metaphors to give a reader information quickly through a word picture*
3. *Metaphor as a way of thinking about objects*

---

4 Metaphor as Disguise

Introduction: This exercise will supplement an understanding of metaphor as a way of speaking of one thing in terms of another. It will also give a young writer a way to express ideas she may feel uneasy about expressing in a more direct form.

Prewriting activity: Have the writer make a list, or tell you a list which you write down, of a number of things or activities she dislikes. Then ask her to tell you who or what other than she herself might decide to do something about the disliked thing. The wind, for instance, might decide to clean its room once and for all or the rabbits might decide to eat all the carrots or the garbage men might decide to fill the garbage cans with cement.

Writing activity: Ask the writer to write a poem in which a disliked activity is taken away by someone or something.

Note: Since the child is being encouraged in this writing activity to express her feelings about something she dislikes doing, it is important that the adult helping the child *not* remind her that everyone must do activities she dislikes. Such admonitions will only reinforce the idea in the writer's mind that a writer should write only about what she likes. This would interfere with writing development.

Skills and Concepts Being Taught:

1. Form in writing gives a writer some distance from emotion so that emotion can be looked at, expressed and shared with a reader
2. Concept that negative feelings are important in writing just as positive feelings are
3. Metaphor as a formal device to be used not only to make a piece of writing visual but also to provide a writer a way of expressing what she may find difficult to express without use of metaphors

5 Developing Contemplation in a Young Writer

Introduction: For a child to write an essay or a story or a poem which is not simply a response to external stimulus, he needs to have time to consider how he feels about an experience and to understand that active consideration of a subject for writing improves the piece of writing. The following activity is designed to promote contemplation of a subject for writing.

Prewriting activity: On a day when you would normally plan a "Fact-Finding Trip," plan instead a trip to a place which will be especially interesting to a child and one which will arouse a child's feelings, such as a zoo, a planetarium, a botanical garden, a natural history museum or an art gallery. Give the young writer a small notebook and say that he may want to write down notes as he walks along. You need not stress note-taking as an activity. What will be important is setting the pace of the trip to meet the child's interests. If he wants to look at the arrowheads at the museum for half an hour, give him time. Answer his questions but avoid giving facts which he doesn't ask for. It is important, too, not to suggest what emotional reaction you have to what you see.

Writing activity: At home, give the writer a notebook and suggest that he write or dictate to you anything he felt or thought about the trip. Tell him that, often, as time passes, feelings and thoughts about something can change and that it might be interesting to make a diary about his thoughts and feelings about the trip over a period of days. Pick a specific time of the day and suggest that he record at that time the next day his thoughts and feelings about the trip and compare them with those already recorded. To stimulate this activity, you may want to ask questions, such as "I

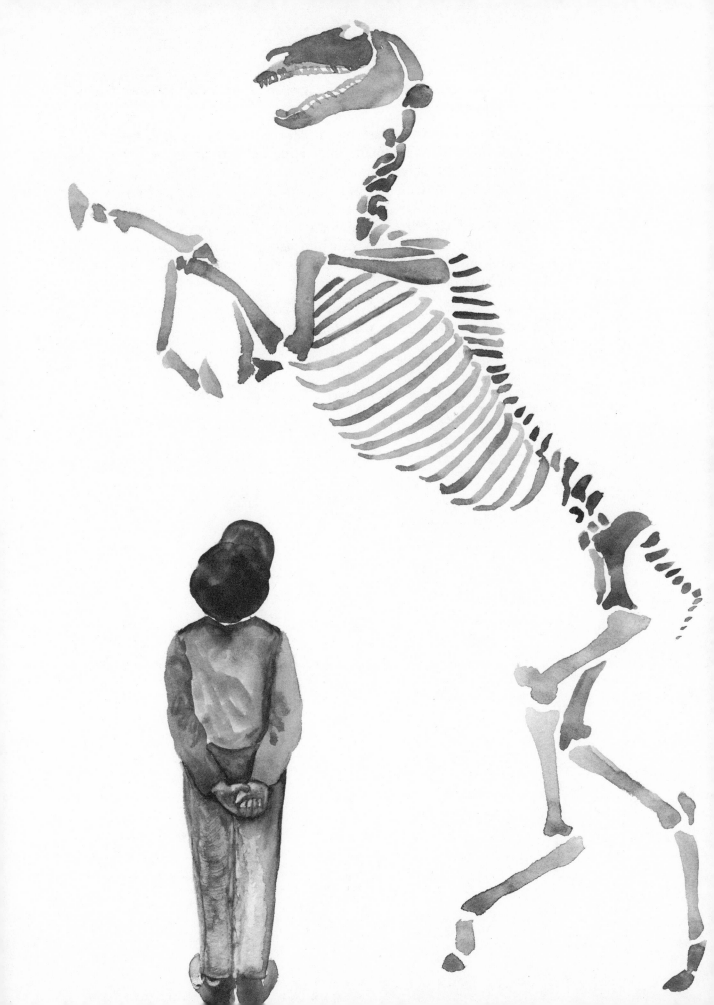

wonder what it's like at night in a museum when everyone's gone home?"

When the writer has several days' entries in the trip diary, tell him that it might be interesting to write about what it's like to think about something over a period of time. Ask such questions as "Do you remember some things and forget others?" and "Why do you remember one thing and forget another?" Give the writer examples of things you think of over and over and talk with him about how it feels to you to think of something often, in various circumstances and at different times.

Skills and Concepts Being Taught:

1. *Memory as a skill used in writing*
2. *Time for thought as a factor in writing*
3. *Writing as a record of extended thinking*
4. *Expository writing*
5. *Use of notes or diary entries as preparation for expository writing*

6 Revision After Contemplation

Introduction: One reason writers revise is that they have changed a small bit as people during the writing of something—the act of writing itself and the thought involved in the act of writing can cause a writer to understand something more clearly. Writers also think about what they have written even after completing a piece of writing. The following activity is designed to help a young writer understand that she changes continually and that she may want to revise a piece of writing done in the past in order to have it reflect who she is now.

Prewriting activity: Ask the young writer to get out her *Book About Me* and read it alone or to you. Ask her if she has changed since writing the book. Ask her to read the book a second time and talk about the specific differences between what is in the text of the book and what is different in her life now.

Writing activity: Ask the young writer to look at each sentence and paragraph in the *Book About Me* and decide if big or small changes need to be made in order to bring the book "up to date." If the changes are small, ask her to rewrite the book, inserting changes. If the changes are extensive, ask if it would be better to write a new *Book About Me* and let the old one stand as a personal record. Suggest that it would be interesting to make a new *Book About Me* every six months or so, in order for the writer to be able to look back and read about herself as she has changed and developed.

Skills and Concepts Being Taught:

1. *Revision or rewriting as a way to express the fact that writing helps a writer understand ideas and feelings better—revision can include new ideas which have resulted from the writing process*
2. *Concept that writing can be a record of a writer's thoughts and feelings*
3. *Differences between revision and rewriting*

7 Metaphorical Writing Following a Trip

Introduction: Young writers are often unaware of how much visual information they have absorbed during an excursion and, unless encouraged to do otherwise, will write down only facts and a few feelings about a trip. This exercise will help a young writer understand how much he has absorbed while looking at something new.

Prewriting activity: After taking the writer to a place he hasn't visited before, divide a piece of paper into two columns, one in which to record his feelings about what he has seen and one in which to draw or write the facts he relates. Ask the writer to tell you about the trip and, as he talks, place his responses in the appropriate columns. Ask questions: how big, what color, who uses it, what happens when it rains, etc.—questions appropriate to the subject. Draw or help or encourage the writer to draw what he has seen and to talk about his feelings.

Writing activity: Give the writer the piece of paper you both have worked on and ask him to write, first, a report of the trip. After he reads his writing, ask if writing a poem about the trip would change the report into a more interesting piece of writing. Encourage him to write such a poem, using some of the information on the "work sheet" and inventing new material as well.

Since the writer will probably use metaphors in the poem, have him point them out to you. Wonder aloud if he used any metaphors in the report and help him search through the report looking for metaphors. Ask the writer to consider if any material in the poem would improve the report and talk about where revisions could be made.

Skills and Concepts Being Taught:

1. Use of a worksheet as preparation for writing
2. Differences between the informative writing in a report and the impressionistic writing in a poem
3. Use of details in impressionistic writing to make report writing more visually interesting

The creature's ribs swelled like a huge cage!

8 What Is Poetry?

Introduction: Poetry is difficult to define, and the young poet can help define it since she has probably been writing poetry for some time now. This exercise in "defining" poetry will help a young writer understand that the writing a writer *does* and the *way* she does it are the keys to defining any form. For this exercise you will need to have books of children's poetry on hand and to ask the young writer to get out the folders containing all the poetry she has written.

Prewriting activity: Sit with the writer and read her poems aloud as well as selections from books of poetry you have. Read poems that rhyme and poems that don't. Talk with the writer about what she notices in the poems: the way they look on the page, what they are about, what feelings they evoke, devices such as simile and metaphor and repetition.

Writing activity: Get a big piece of paper or poster board and have the writer write down, in a list, ways of using language that make written work be a poem. Help the writer with suggestions: Poetry is more than just facts about something. What makes it "more"? Can poems be funny? Suggest: Let's see how many different feelings we can find in the poems you've written. Ask: Could you write a poem about writing a poem?

Skills and Concepts Being Taught:

1. *Concept that particular forms in writing—the poem, the story, the report—are defined by* writers using form *and not by "rules"*
2. *Careful reading in order to notice various devices in writing*
3. *Writing itself as a subject for writing*
4. *Identifying emotions within poetry*

---

9 A Book About Poetry

Introduction: The young writer or writers you have been working with have, by now, written probably dozens of poems, stories and various reports and essays. In exercise 8, the writer has discovered how much knowledge about writing poetry he has accumulated. This exercise is designed to combine knowledge and interest in poetry with work on academic skills, specifically those required for writing a long and complex piece of nonfiction.

Prewriting activity: Ask the child to gather together in one place all the writing and books, including the list about poetry from exercise 8, that he has accumulated. Tell the writer that he has learned a lot about poetry that others may not know, especially children, and that it would be interesting if he wrote a book *about* poetry for other children who may not have yet learned so much. Tell him that you can help but that it's an important kind of writing which will require some planning. Ask the child to tell you, after looking through all the gathered material, how he might organize such a book. As he talks, draw on paper a "picture," by blocking out sections, of the book. Ask such questions as: Will you want to give examples of similes and metaphors? Will you want to give an overall introduction, using the list about poetry we made previously? and so on. As you draw a "picture" of the book's organization, talk about it with the writer. Since the organization at this point will probably not be substantial, ask him if it would help to read over his poems and to remember how he came to understand poetry writing. Suggest that he make a list of the writing processes he has learned. Ask if he would use exercises in the book or lists of ideas for poetry. As the writer considers the organization of the book, take notes or have him take them. Tell the writer that all the possibilities for organization can be considered and that later he can "draw" a master plan. Ask if he feels it would help to consult other books about poetry or if he wants to write only about his experiences and knowledge about poetry.

Give the writer a set of note cards, a piece of poster board, and a set of variously colored pens. Provide plenty of work space which can remain undisturbed for a number of days or weeks. Ask occasionally how the project of organization is going and answer any questions he may have.

Writing activity: When it appears that the young writer has decided upon what he wants to go into the book and how it is to be organized, remind him that revisions can be made during the writing. Suggest that he begin writing an introduction, to be followed by various chapters. Exclaim over progress of the book. If the writer says he is encountering problems, ask what they are and offer to help solve them. Tell him that errors can be corrected later.

Skills and Concepts Being Taught:

1. *Concept that writing can be a subject for writing*
2. *Organizational skills*
3. *Using previously completed writing to produce new writing*
4. *Information-gathering; analysis of information*
5. *Memory as a tool in writing*
6. *Note-taking as a tool in writing*
7. *Library research as a tool in writing*
8. *Revision*

---

10 Helping Young Writers Correct Errors

Introduction: *When* a child is ready to learn the conventions of English which relate to spelling, grammar, and punctuation is individual for each child. Much harm can be done to a writer just beginning her explorations of language by a severe focus on the conventions. Teaching conventional usage should *never* become more important than what a child has to say. A first-grader telling a story will often string events together with *and*s in her excitement over the story. When the same child writes, she is very busy trying to "catch" in writing—still physically difficult due to the degree of manual dexterity involved—as much of what is going through her mind as possible. This child would be unduly burdened by being told that periods or question marks should come at the end of sentences. Anyone teaching writing to a child will need to pay close attention to that child in order to determine when she is ready to be taught conventional practices.

There are several games that are useful.

1. Since young writers like to "decorate" their writing with drawings, you can point out that printed books have a kind of "picture" after sets of words. Draw, then, on paper a period, a question mark, an exclamation mark. Write out a question, such as "Who are you?" Ask the writer to imagine that the question mark is a dull sort of picture which could be more interesting. Say that it could be, for instance, a picture of a person standing on tiptoe with his hands curved over his head, waiting for an answer. Have the child write a question and then a question mark made more interesting as a picture but still resembling a question mark. Ask her to ask a number of questions and to feel her voice "rise" at the

end. Tell the writer that when she has finished a piece of writing and is reading it over, she might like to "draw" question marks at the end of words which cause the voice to "rise." Later, make similar suggestions about periods and exclamation marks.

2. A "spelling bee," with several children or adults (with adults getting words sufficiently difficult for misspellings), made into a game *separate* from the creative process of writing can be helpful.

3. A child can make her own dictionary, putting in it, on blank sheets with letters at the top to designate sections, any words she knows how to spell. Do not be disturbed if the child adds misspelled words; simply ask her to read the dictionary to you. In pencil, in small letters, you can write above the child's word the correct spelling, explaining simply that you spell the word a bit differently and that you're putting your spelling above the word so that you'll remember next time what it is.

4. Once a week, you can talk with a child about two or three errors in her writing. At this time it is important to judge the child's attitude and your own: she should be interested in talking about her writing and you should feel relaxed and nonjudgmental.

5. When a writer is preparing a book for "publication," you can suggest that you and she talk about who the book is for and what will make the experience of reading the book most enjoyable for the reader. At that time, you can suggest proper spelling just as you would talk about illustrations and binding for the book. If the stories have dialogue in them, it may be appropriate to talk about the use of quotation marks or paragraphing.

6. Third- through sixth-graders often like to make up stories and poems about how punctuation is used or about a misspelled word who got lost because he looked different than he usually did. You can suggest such titles as "The Question Mark Who Ran Away," "The Twins Who Went Everywhere Together" (for a colon), etc.

7. Help a young writer learn to enjoy a dictionary by sitting with her and reading it just as you would a story, talking about the different meanings for a word and trying to make up sentences for the different meanings.

8. If the writer is being taught how to write a bibliographic entry for a term paper, ask her if she would like to invent books written by and about famous people or television and popular music personalities and write them in a similar form.

9. Suggest that a young writer make specialized lists of words which she can write as pictures to indicate by the way the words are written the feelings associated with the words: happy words, funny words, scary words, noisy words, quiet words, etc. Help her spell the words properly before the "drawing" begins by suggesting she look up the word in the dictionary to see if it has any interesting letters she may have forgotten.

10. Make a list of the common words the writer most often misspells. Write each of the words vertically down a page and suggest that she make a special poetry folder titled "Poems from First Letters." Suggest that she write poems for all the words, with each line beginning with one of the letters: S
      U
      N
      N
      Y

Skills and Concepts Being Taught:

1. Punctuation as an integral part of sentences, a part a writer can visualize
2. Spelling as a skill
3. Revision of errors as a natural and interesting part of writing
4. Concept of a reader or an audience
5. Concept that standardized spelling and use of punctuation helps a reader
6. Concept that words are often associated with specific feelings

---

11 Learning to Organize from Activity

Introduction: Organized writing is similar to organized play or work—one element comes first because what follows will be easier to do or more enjoyable. The following suggestions will lead a young writer to understand that well-organized writing has a logic to it.

Prewriting activity: Tell the writer that you think it might be fun to write some descriptions of activities that a person from another planet, for instance, might find puzzling upon first encountering them. Suggest that he help you choose a few very common activities that such a stranger might like to read about. You could suggest making cookies, setting the table, making a phone call, making a bed, tying a shoe, etc. As you or the writer performs one of the tasks, ask him to make a list of each object used, each movement as if it were filmed in slow motion, and, with a stop watch, if necessary, the amount of time each part of the activity takes. Tell him to list everything he can about the activity. Then ask him to take scissors and cut apart the items into segments or blocks which indicate beginning, middle, and end, or other appropriate segments. As you read the list with the writer, ask if the stranger would want to know why the activity is done or anything about its history. Ask if people's feelings about the activity should be included. Make additions to the list as needed.

Writing exercise: Ask the writer to take the parts of the list to a table and, using the list as a guide, to write a description to the stranger in such a way that he, she, or "it" could understand the activity.

Reinforcement activity:
1. When the writer has finished a description, have him read it as you "pretend" to be the stranger. Repeat the description as if you had no previous knowledge of the activity. Ask the writer if you have understood it correctly.
2. Ask the writer to look at his Map of an Imaginary Place in order to discover if the inhabitants of the place play any unfamiliar games, eat anything unfamiliar, wear clothes different from his, etc. Ask him to describe one of the different activities in such a way as to make it understandable to people in his school or town.

Skills and Concepts Being Taught:

1. *Descriptive writing*
2. *Concept of a reader or audience*
3. *Methods of gathering information*
4. *Organization of information*
5. *Concept that feelings as well as facts give information*
6. *Information-gathering as preparation for a piece of writing*

12 From Letters to Essays

Introduction: The following activities will encourage a young writer to move from one form of writing into another and to think of writing as a response to other writing.

Prewriting activity: At the library, help the writer choose a book about a historical period prior to the invention of the telephone. After you and she read the book, talk with her about communication before the telephone, the computer, television and radio, etc. With the writer, go through the text picking out situations in which important information needed to be communicated from one person to another or to several people. Make a list (as exhaustive as possible) of what probably needed to be communicated and to whom. Talk with her about the form of letters and the differences between notes to friends and formal letters to others. Discuss the difference between letters meant to convey feelings and letters designed to give or ask for information.

Writing activity: Ask the writer to decide on a period of time she wants to write letters about and to whom and from whom the letters will come. Suggest that some should be letters giving or asking for information and some might be to friends about how the letter writer feels about events. Give her several different sizes of paper and suggest that she write, in letter form, a "history" of a part of the event.

Second writing activity: After the writer has a "history" in letters, ask her to imagine how the historical event might have gone differently had the participants had telephones and other modern means of communication. Suggest that she write an essay about how the event might have changed as a result of modern communication.

Third writing activity: Ask the writer to imagine that one of the main participants in the event decided in old age to write his memories about the event, including facts and feelings. Suggest that she imaginatively "become" that main participant and write the memory.

Skills and Concepts Being Taught:

1. Concept that information about something can come from a variety of sources
2. Differences between formal and informal writing
3. Feelings as well as facts give information
4. Close attention to reading as a method of gaining information
5. Reading as a stimulus for writing
6. Concept that history is affected by methods of communication
7. Using several forms of writing to communicate similar information

13 The Writer Becomes an Editor

Introduction: This exercise can be used with the child's book about poetry or with any piece of prose, fiction or nonfiction, the child has written. The exercise can be enjoyable with one writer or a group of writers. What is important is to give the writer the sense that editing a piece of writing is a natural part of the writing process and is important work. Tell him that many professional writers do nothing but edit the work of other writers. Provide work space, a book about rules of English, a dictionary, and several pencils with colored ink.

Exercise: Ask the writer to choose a piece of writing he has written and especially likes. Ask him to make a list of techniques he will look at in the writing. You may suggest paragraphing, sentence structure, choice of words, overall organization, punctuation, spelling. Suggest that he look at each element separately. Tell him that it may be good to cut the writing apart with scissors so that new language can be inserted. Look through the English handbook with the writer to help him understand how to find answers to questions about grammar, punctuation, etc. Be available to answer questions. What is helpful to the writer is, first, giving him the sense that the activity is important and can be enjoyable, and, second, avoiding any criticism of his errors. In answering questions, say, "Let's see if we can find an answer for that in one of your books." If the writer finds the work tedious, suggest he put it away until he feels fresher. Avoid pushing him to edit but show interest in the process.

Editing with a group of writers: Editing can be especially enjoyable for young writers when they work as a group, consulting with each other. Allow the group of writers to work independent of adult supervision—the editing work need not be perfect. A process is being taught, and that is more important here than whether or not the writing is "correct." A family group can work, too, if family members

are involved in editing as an activity of *asking questions*:
what does the writer mean to say?, what does the writing
actually say?, what can be done to make what the writer
means to say come out in words?, and what about spelling,
grammar, and punctuation?

Skills and Concepts Being Taught:

1. *Editing a piece of writing can be an
   interesting and enjoyable activity*
2. *Use of the dictionary and grammar handbook
   in editing*
3. *Paying close attention to writing*
4. *Concept of a reader or audience for writing*

14 Methods of Research

Introduction: Research can be done in a library but also in the "field"—where new information can be found. This exercise will provide a writer with an opportunity to do research at home and to use the research as a basis for writing. It will also give the writer an opportunity to make use of her "All About My Home" map as a basis for research and writing.

Prewriting activity: Ask the writer to get out her "All About My Home" map. As you look at the map with her, talk about the fact that people living closely together often become so accustomed to each other and the place where they live that they don't realize how much is happening in one place. Suggest that it would be interesting and informative for the writer to do research on what happens in her home. Ask such questions as: How many meals do we eat a week at the table? How much television do we watch and what do we watch? How many books do we own, and how many do we get from the library each week? How far is it from each person's bed to the bathroom, to the kitchen, etc.? On the average, how often does the telephone ring each week, and how often do we call from the home? Looking at the map with the writer, help her list categories of needed information on file cards. Suggest that she begin gathering information in each category. Talk with the writer about how she would like to gather information, suggesting that she devise a method.

Writing activity: When the writer has decided she has finished gathering information, talk with her about what she has discovered. Suggest that it would be interesting to write a report about what happens in the home for others in the family to read. Talk with her about how the material could be organized, helping her to separate the file cards into categories: food, television-viewing habits, reading habits, etc. Talk with her about an introduction to the research paper, suggesting that a research report might give the reader information about how the research was conducted, over what period of time, etc. Suggest that she begin writing the report, adding that pictures and graphs may be useful. Tell her that you will be happy to help if she needs assistance. Provide any materials the writer discovers she needs.

Editing reinforcement activity: When her research report has gone through the first draft, ask the writer to share it with you, saying that it would be interesting to "publish" it as a book, as a family record. As the writer talks with you about the writing, ask her what she thinks should be done with the material to prepare it for publication. Go over each page with her, first expressing overall interest. As you observe spelling errors and grammar and punctuation errors, mention a very few to the writer and ask if she would like to correct them for publication. If she is not interested in correcting errors, do not insist. If she wants errors corrected, talk with her about how she would like to accomplish that. You may, if the writer wants to correct errors, suggest that the material might make a more attractive book if copied on heavier paper and that, if the writing is to be recopied, errors could be corrected with a red pencil on the original material. Begin copy editing spelling errors by having the writer bring the dictionary to the work table; help her look up the misspelled words. For grammar and punctuation errors, ask her to get her English handbook and help her use it. Do a small amount of copy editing at a time so that the writer will not lose enthusiasm.

Skills and Concepts Being Taught:

1. Concept that research for a piece of writing is an important part of writing
2. Organization of information in preparation for writing
3. Concept that a reader of a piece of informational writing may be helped by understanding the writer's research methods
4. Report-writing based on research
5. Editing as a part of the writing process

15 Making Stories More Complete

Introduction: Young writers' minds often work far too quickly for their hands to follow in writing. When young writers write stories, they often write only the action, with very little description of place and of characters' feelings. They feel a need to round out a story by coming to a conclusion, which contributes to the omission of story elements other than plot. Too, very young writers have a difficult time imagining an audience; therefore, they often do not understand that what they "see" is often not put on the paper. There is no way to "force" a young writer to imagine a reader for his story, but it is possible to encourage young writers to include elements of the story beyond the plot. The following game will help a young writer become accustomed to elements of the story form which enrich stories.

The story game: Cut a circle from cardboard and punch a hole in its center. With a felt-tip pen, divide the circle into three equal triangles. Make an arrow from cardboard and attach it to the circle with a fastener so that the arrow spins. Using masking tape (so that the circle can be reused), write on it the names of three story characters you have asked the child to invent. Next, on a stack of cards, write the words "description of place," "mood," "dialogue," "action," "description of person." Make ten cards with "mood" on them, ten with "action" on them, etc. Shuffle the cards. Tell the child that you will take turns spinning the wheel. When the arrow lands on a character's name, the person whose turn it is will draw a card from the face-down stack and tell about the character in relation to the card: "Henry" and "mood" would require that the player talk about Henry's mood. If the next player spins the arrow to "Terry" and picks up a "description of a person" card, he would describe Terry. It will be natural for the characters to interact as each player takes his turn and a story will begin to develop which interrelates all three characters. When all the cards have been used, each player can have one more "round." On the final play, each person should choose one card from the stack, either "action," "mood," "description of place," "dialogue." He may then place the arrow on the character he chooses and "finish" the story. The next player adds a second ending which fits with the first ending.

Story game writing activity: After a story has been made by the players, ask the writer if he would like to write it out, changing it any way he likes, using the story board or not. You may also want to tape record the game and play back the story invented from the game. As the recording plays, you can talk with the writer about how the story is "weak" in some places, "silly" in others, and talk about how the story could be improved.

Skills and Concepts Being Taught:

1. *Concept that stories are enriched by description and dialogue*
2. *Expanding upon plot in story writing*
3. *A verbal word game can provide material for writing*
4. *Revision in story writing*

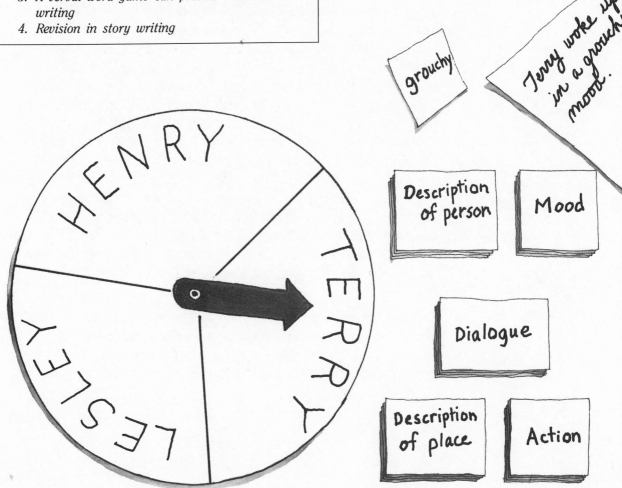

16 Research by Interviewing

Introduction: Young writers learn that writing usually involves planning if they routinely engage in activities which are preparations for writing. The following exercise is designed to give a writer practice in prewriting planning and in another method of research as preparation for the writing of an essay.

Preparation: Talk with the writer about the fact that most people have interesting experiences which others don't get to know about because no one has asked and written down the experiences for others to read. Mention some of your own experiences which you have not written about but which are, for example, a part of a national history, such as how the death of a President or the first moon walk affected you. Also mention that many people do interesting jobs but that others often don't know what is involved in doing the jobs. How, for instance, does the mailman know where to deliver all the letters in his or her satchel? Suggest that the writer think about something she would like to know about and which someone in the neighborhood could explain. When she has chosen a topic and a person who knows about the topic, talk with her about the questions she might ask. Tell the writer that sometimes people don't always tell all the facts unless asked questions that are specific. Help her prepare a list of questions. Ask if time of day might be important or the weather or how the person doing the job or recalling an event feels or felt at the time, etc. When a series of questions has been listed, ask the writer if the order in which the questions are asked is important. Suggest that she might want to organize her questions before doing the interview.

Talk with the writer about how quickly many people talk and ask if she wants to consider how to write down what the person being interviewed says. Give her a divided stenographer's pad and suggest that she may want to make headings on each side of the paper or other identifications as preparation for having to write quickly.

The interviewing process: Suggest that the writer set up a time for one or two interviews and begin gathering information. When she has done the first interview, talk with her about the material she obtained and ask her what other information she would need if she were to write about the material. Ask if she needs to get information from the library as "background" or any facts to make the material more easily understood. Suggest that she prepare for a second interview if it seems necessary for a complete report.

Note: This exercise can be used with even very young writers since the focus of the exercise is on a process of planning and on the adult and the child talking about how a writer gathers information for writing. A very young writer could, for instance, interview a grandparent about how cooking was done before microwaves, grills, broilers, blenders, etc., came into use or about what people did for entertainment before television became popular.

Skills and Concepts Being Taught:

1. *Interviewing as a method of doing research*
2. *Organization as a preparation for conducting an interview*
3. *Time and place as factors in people's lives that influence facts*
4. *Organization by ordering material into categories which indicate significant and less significant facts*
5. *Skill of interviewing*
6. *Library research as an aid in preparing for an interview*
7. *Assessing material gathered during an interview*

17 Writing an Essay from an Interview

(1st- and 2nd-graders may need help with writing)

Introduction: For this writing activity, it is important for the writer to decide when he is prepared to write the essay. He may become interested in expanding the interviewing process to include interviews with additional people in order to gain a broader perspective on a subject. A very young writer may want to write the essay after only one brief interview. Your role is simply to show interest in the material and to suggest that the writer tear from the steno pad all the pages from the interview for the purpose of surveying the material for organization.

Prewriting activity: Tell the writer that an essay is *about* a topic and that material from the interview can be incorporated into the essay in two ways: summary of material gained in an interview and direct quotation of what the person who was interviewed said. Talk with him about introductory paragraphs which give the reader an indication about what will be in the body of the essay and help him organize the material. Tell him that, after a first draft is written, he may want to reorganize the writing by cutting it into sections with scissors and rearranging it. Stress that in a first draft a writer does not need to organize everything "perfectly" since a draft is writing to work with just as material from an interview is writing to work with. Encourage him to begin writing.

Writing activity: Suggest that the writer begin a draft of the essay. When it appears that he has a section of the essay written, show interest in it and ask him to read it to you. Comments such as "That's very interesting!" and "What comes next?" are appropriate, but refrain from suggesting revisions. A very young writer using this exercise will write sentences strung together with *and*. The interview will be summarized in repetition: "He said that." Avoid criticism of these practices and encourage the writer to continue.

Note: A writer's work on second and third drafts may or may not follow the exercise immediately. Allow him to decide how much rewriting he wants to do immediately following the writing of a first draft. It would be helpful for you to show interest in what has been written. You may ask if the writer wants to show the essay to the person he interviewed and, if so, ask if it is ready for an audience, a reader.

A very young writer, either writing his own essay or dictating it, will "revise" verbally as it is read aloud. You will help the writer by saying, "That's interesting! Do you want to add what you just said to your essay?"

Skills and Concepts Being Taught:

1. Using material gathered during an interview in the writing of an essay
2. Difference between writing which summarizes information gained during an interview and information given in direct quotation
3. Organization in writing
4. Revision in writing
5. Concept of a reader or audience for a piece of writing

18 The Reader or Audience for Writing

Introduction: The younger the writer, the greater the difficulty she has in stepping back from a piece of writing and imagining how it will be understood by a reader. The following game will help writers of any age place themselves in a reader's position.

The game: Get from the library a number of books, both fiction and nonfiction, which the child has not read. Sit with her and, covering with a piece of paper all but the first few paragraphs, read or have her read to you the opening paragraphs of the book. Tell the child that since neither of you knows what will come next in the text, you will take turns reading the paragraphs over and guessing what the writer of the book will tell you next. As each of you "guesses," talk about how you made a decision, what words are giving you clues. On a note pad or verbally, list what each player thinks will be next. Then read the text for several more paragraphs, giving points to the player who correctly "guessed" what the writer wrote. You may want to underline clue words if you are using books which the child owns and has not yet read. An older writer may want to write out a book's beginning in widely spaced lines and write above various words what information about forthcoming words she is getting from specific words. Play the game as often as the child shows interest in it.

Skills and Concepts Being Taught:

1. *Every word in a piece of writing conveys information*
2. *Writing is organized*
3. *Paying close attention to words in sentences and to sentences as they convey information sequentially*
4. *Imaginative thinking within the confines of a specific piece of writing*

---

19 Concrete Poetry

Introduction: This exercise extends a writer's understanding of poetry as both words and shape, and emphasizes work with poetic form the writer encountered when working on the "All About Me" exercise in Part I. In *concrete poems* the words are put on the page to illustrate the subject or feeling of the poem. For example, a poem *about* a willow tree can be put on the page with lines hanging down like dozens of limbs drooping with leaves and with a trunk of words.

Prewriting activity: Ask the writer if he would like to write some "concrete" poems and explain what concrete poetry is. Suggest that he can either sketch a shape and then fill it with words, later erasing the lines making up the drawing, or write the words *as* a drawing. Suggest a few topics and shapes; suggest that the writer get out his "All About Me" exercise and see if he has written any concrete poems on it.

Writing activity: Have the writer write several concrete poems.

Note: You may want to talk with the writer about the fact that in many books of science and history and in many textbooks, prose is often segmented into "pictures" when information is given in lists, in diagrams, etc. Ask the writer to look at several textbooks and notice groups of words being segregated from the main text into "pictures" to help readers "see" sets of facts.

Skills and Concepts Being Taught:

1. *Poetry can be shaped in many different ways*
2. *Pictures can be made from words and the arrangement of words on a page in order to enhance a poem's meaning*
3. *How words are arranged on a page affects how a reader gains information in all types of writing*

20 Vocabulary-Building Simile Poem Using Synonyms

Grades 3-9

Introduction: This exercise is designed to help writers appreciate the wealth of visual images which attach themselves to different ways of saying something, and it reinforces the use of similes as a way to make writing more visual. The exercise also teaches use of synonyms.

Prewriting exercise: On a large poster board, write a common action verb such as *walk* or *talk*. Talk with the writer about the many ways people, animals, insects can walk, suggesting stroll, amble, inch, etc. Suggest that a book of synonyms would probably contain a number of different words which can be substituted for *walk* and help the writer use the synonym dictionary. On the poster board, with the word *walk* as the hub of a wheel, write different words for *walk* coming away from the "hub" like spokes on a tire. After you and the child have made a "word wheel," talk with her about one of the words, such as *mosey*. Tell her that it would be fun to make phrases using similes to describe in more detail what it means to mosey, such as the phrases "He moseyed into town like a cowboy on Saturday night" or "She moseyed to the blackboard like a cow."

Writing activity: Give the writer a set of colored pens and suggest that she write similes to go with each synonym.

Skills and Concepts Being Taught:

1. *Using synonyms*
2. *Making writing visual*
3. *Extending the visual aspect of a word by using similes*
4. *Concept that there are many ways of saying something and that writing suggests ideas for new writing*

---

plod

slither

walk

strut

hop

creep

21 Words Reveal How We Feel

Introduction: The similes the writer has used in Exercise 20 probably demonstrate that he understands that different words suggest different feelings. This exercise focuses on feelings commonly connected to various words and will help a young writer understand that a writer does not use synonyms arbitrarily but chooses particular words to convey feeling. The exercise also reinforces storytelling.

Prewriting activity: Ask the writer to play a word/action game with you. Tell him that you will give him a word and that he should try to demonstrate through action what the word suggests. Say, "If I say *eat,* would you show me a person eating?" Follow that with, "When I say *wolf down food,* show me what it looks like." Continue the game with various words such as: *pick at, gobble, devour, inhale, snack, graze, chomp, nibble, mush,* etc.

Writing activity: Suggest that the writer write a story about a pie-eating contest. Ask him first to decide what characters will be in the contest and to give them names. Then tell him that it would be interesting to have the story focus on how these characters normally eat when they are at home and how they decide to eat when trying to win a pie-eating contest. Suggest that the writer may want to consult the synonym dictionary for additional words for eating other than those you and he have talked about. Give the writer different colored pens and suggest that he change pens in order to "color" different words describing eating.

Skills and Concepts Being Taught:

1. *Synonyms not used arbitrarily but to convey specific information*
2. *Sense of place in writing affects information a reader gets about a character or person being written about*
3. *Visual writing*
4. *Using similes*

---

22 Giving a Story's Main Character Personality

Introduction: It is important to help young writers understand that completing a piece of writing sometimes takes a long time. A writer must often "build" a story or essay from bits and pieces of writing—something like an architect beginning with numerous sketches. This exercise is designed to help young writers understand that stories and their plots often grow from a writer's developing interest in a character.

Prewriting exercise: Say to the writer, "Let's talk about a person we'll invent, make up out of our imaginations." When the writer responds—no matter what she begins with—follow the response with a question. Continue the question-and-answer session until you and the child are in a conversation about an invented person. Then ask her to get a large sheet of paper so that you and she may record a few facts about the character: age, type of shoes the character wears in the house, favorite food, best friend, neighbors, etc. When the character has accumulated a "full" life, ask the writer to get a second sheet of paper and to sketch a map similar to the maps made in Part I exercises. As she begins to sketch on the map the main character's house and town, show interest by asking questions such as "Does she (or he) ever go to the library (or sports arena or ice cream shop, etc.)? By now the main character will have a name—use it when asking about him or her.

When the writer says the map is finished, ask her to show it to you and tell you about an ordinary day in the main character's life. Then ask, "If the main character had something happen to change him or her *and* what happened *didn't* come from outside town, such as a tornado or a stranger coming to town, what might that something be?

Look at the map with the writer and talk about what unusual event might happen: a neighbor's dog bit the postman, for instance. When the writer chooses the event, ask her to get the list of facts she made about the main character and to look at it along with the map. Talk with her about how a person reacts to unusual events in a way that is peculiar to him or her because of personal likes, dislikes, fears, habits, etc. Ask her to think about the small ways in which a person reacts to change.

Writing activity: Suggest to the writer that she probably has a great deal of knowledge about the main character now and could write a story about the main character in such a way that someone reading the story would know the character and how he or she behaves when something unusual happens. Give her plenty of paper and a number of pens and tell her that you would be very interested in reading the story, adding, "Of course you know so much about _____ that it may take some time for you to tell what makes him (or her) do what he (or she) will do when something unusual happens. You may want to write the story in parts."

most comfortable → shoes

best ↗ cap

favorite ↗ wild animal

Note: This activity may be used with very young writers if the exercise is worked at over a period of days. A "game-like" atmosphere could help stimulate interest—simply say, "I wonder what _____ is doing today? Go get your materials and let's find out." Very young writers, of course, may want help with writing or prefer to give dictation.

Skills and Concepts Being Taught:

1. Collecting detailed, imagined material for a story.
2. Preparing to write a story by imagining details about a main character's life
3. Visualization as an aid to imaginative writing
4. Concept that action in a story derives from the personalities of characters
5. Writing a long story in parts so that the writer can control the material

biggest fear ↓

← favorite junk food

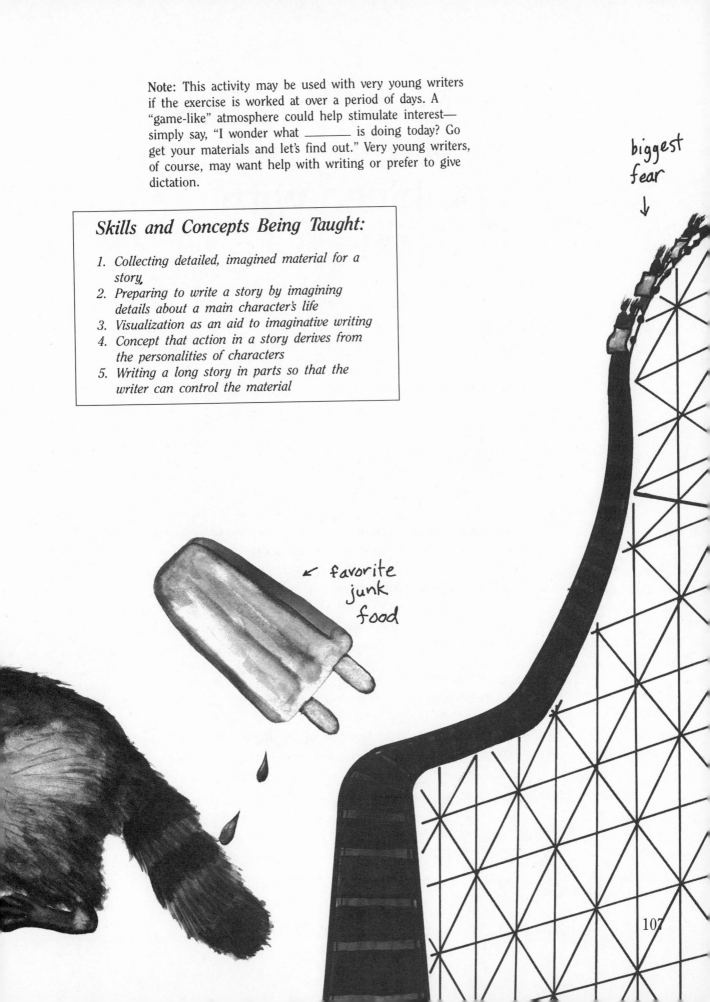

23 Writing Stimulated by Writing and Combined with Revision

Introduction: A young writer can come to understand and appreciate revision as a natural part of writing when both the excitement and the frustration of using written language are incorporated into a writing game. Tell the writer that you want to play a writing game which will require several big sheets of paper and a pair of scissors as well as two different-colored pens. Assemble the materials.

The game: Ask the child to write a sentence, any sentence, on the paper with the pen of his choice and say that you will follow with a sentence of your own that will in some way relate to the first sentence. Take turns making up sentences with the writer, using the colored pen the child isn't using. When the story or poem or essay seems to have come to some conclusion, tell the writer that it's a collaboration which would be totally different if each of you had written the story, poem, or essay alone. Ask him to separate the sentences with scissors into two stacks: "Yours" and "Mine." Say, "Let's each read our stacks and see what we've got—we can arrange the lines in any order we want. But what if I want one of your lines? Can we trade? Or should we add new lines of our own?" Let him decide how the game should proceed next, either by trading lines, adding new lines, or doing both. When each of you have a new piece of writing, read to each other. Repeat the game as long as the child enjoys playing.

Skills and Concepts Being Taught:

1. *Concept that a writer often decides what he wants to write about* while *writing*
2. *Revision*
3. *Using writing to stimulate new writing*

108

24 What Happens When I Write?

Introduction: Even very young writers are aware that writing is an activity which requires particular skills. It can help a developing writer to write about herself *as a writer* since such analysis encourages the writer to see herself *in charge of writing*. This exercise is designed to help a writer become more conscious of herself as a writer who makes decisions.

Prewriting activity: Ask the writer to talk with you about different ways she feels, different "moods," telling you how each one affects her differently. Encourage her to mention how she reacts to dressing, eating, playing, etc., when in different moods. Then ask the writer to describe the mood she is currently in and to name another mood very different from the current one.

Writing exercise I: Ask the writer to write an essay about the feelings she has chosen as most different from the mood she is now in. Suggest that the writer give the essay a title: "When I Am Sad" (or Angry or Impatient, etc.).

Writing exercise II: When the writer has finished, mention that she has just completed a complex process and talk with her about what it would be like to write about what happens when she is writing. Ask, "Did you have to imagine feeling sad (or lonely or angry)? Did you have to think of specific events and people? How did you decide how to begin?" Suggest that it would be interesting if the writer wrote about how she wrote the essay about a mood she wasn't in at the time of the writing. Say, "Put *everything* you can think of in the essay so that a person who doesn't know how to write could get an idea about it from reading the essay."

Skills and Concepts Being Taught:

1. *Concept that a writer makes* decisions *about writing and is in* charge *of writing as an activity*
2. *A writer's mood while writing affects writing*
3. *Imagination requires that a writer use memories of moods in order to write about topics which may not coincide with her mood as she is writing*
4. *Writing can be a topic for writing*
5. *Skill of becoming conscious of decisions made during writing*

110

25 Talking to the Author

Introduction: Since every writer composes a piece of writing one sentence at a time, making decisions about writing every step of the way, a young writer can be encouraged to understand that writing is a building process by playing the following game. The game will also help a writer understand the reader as "audience"—that is, the reader, too, gets information from a writer one step at a time by paying attention to the meaning of each word as it relates to other words and as words grow into sentences or lines or paragraphs or stanzas.

The game: Tell the writer that you want to read aloud to him but that you want to stop after every sentence and give him time to say anything he wants to about the sentence (or line of poetry, if you've chosen to play the game with poetry). Tell the writer he may ask questions or make statements but that questions and statements should relate to the writing. Read a line or sentence; let the writer respond, and repeat the process until the piece of writing you have chosen has been read and responded to. Then ask the writer how many ideas or questions he had while you were reading were in the *author's* mind as he or she wrote.

Note: For very young writers, this exercise can be suggested by stopping the reading of a story or poem to ask, "How do you suppose the person who wrote this story or poem knew what to put next? Can you guess?"

Skills and Concepts Being Taught:

1. Concept of the reader or audience for a piece of writing
2. Paying close attention to each word in a sentence
3. Imagining the writer of a piece of writing and imagining the decisions a writer has made to create a piece of writing
4. Organization in writing

26 **Brainstorming**

Children who like to write will discover that writing is a meaningful and satisfying activity which includes elements of both play and learning. Writing as an activity for children can, in other words, come to feel natural to a child as a means of expression. Some children will need very little encouragement to express themselves in writing, but others may need help in deciding what to write. An adult helping such a child can, with a little practice, become adept at helping her discover opportunities for writing. Such expertise is a matter of practice. It is helpful if you "practice" in front of the writer, which is a way of encouraging her to discover opportunities for writing.

Method: Ask, "I wonder if we can think about *what* to write about out of a hundred thousand things? Let's look around." Then pick up something nearby and look at it, turning it over and studying it. Say, "Let's see." Say the name of the object several times slowly, then ask, "Any ideas?" Give the object to the writer and say, "You think of something and then as quickly as I can, I'll think of something. Fast! Anything that comes to mind." Alternate ideas, exclaiming over each one the writer gives. Add a few, "What if . . ." situations—what if, if you're holding a pencil, for instance, no one had invented lead (or paper)? Play the game until the writer feels a sense of amazement at the number of writing topics that can be associated with just one object. Repeat the game with several objects. On other days, you can play the game in a variety of ways. What follows is a list of variations on the game which can suggest topics for writing to a young writer.

1. In turns, go to a window and, looking out to the count of ten, name what you see. Alternate turns with the writer.
2. Start a sentence with, "If I were late for school, I'd . . ." and ask the writer to complete the sentence. Alternate but change the name of the activity a person might be late for: "If I were late to baseball practice . . . ," etc.
3. Begin a sentence by saying, *BIG things*: an elephant."

Repeat *"BIG things:"* and wait for the writer to suggest something big. After several exchanges, change the word "big" for "enormous," then "colossal," etc. On other days, use other words to begin an exchange of lists: things that are soft, silver-colored, smelly, purple, tiny, ripped, etc.

4. Pick up various tools and ask: "What did people use before this was invented?"

5. Say, "I have a favorite number, do you?" Ask why, then talk about why people have feelings about numbers.

6. Ask, "Do you wonder how an elephant got its tail (or a lion its roar, etc.). Suggest the writer invent a reason for an animal's being as it is.

7. Ask the writer to close her eyes. Ask her to describe objects you give her to feel.

8. Practice rhyming with a writer, with each of you seeing who can rhyme one word with others the most times. Ask, then, "What if a word got tired of rhyming? What would it do?"

9. Taking turns, give a color and each of you name as many objects which are that color as you can. Ask the writer if it would be interesting to write a poem or story or essay titled "Yellow" or "Purple."

10. Give the writer a stack of pictures from magazines and ask her to make story titles to go with the pictures.

11. Tell a story with the writer by taking turns, stopping before the story is finished. Ask her to finish the story.

12. Suggest that you and the writer play the "silly questions" game, with each of you asking the silliest questions you can think of. Suggest that stories, poems, and essays can be written about silly questions.

13. Taking turns, play a game with similes, with you beginning by saying, "A tornado is like a _____," with

the writer comparing a tornado to something else. Then ask her to provide a phrase which you are to complete. Suggest that the writer make a poem of ten similes.

14. Suggest that you and the writer make a book of definitions: "Loneliness is . . . ," "Imagination is . . . ," etc. Encourage her to work on the project by expanding it to include many definitions.

15. Suggest that you and the writer alternate turns talking about what you would be if you were different: "If I were a tightrope walker . . . ," etc.

16. Play a memory game by asking the writer to take turns with you trying to remember everything in a particular place.

17. Using a stack of pictures, ask the writer to begin a story by imagining how the objects in the picture got in the picture.

18. Play the "Is Silence Always the Same?" game. Ask the writer to close her eyes. Make a sound and then ask her to describe what the room "sounds" like with the silence gone. Repeat with a variety of sounds.

19. Ask the writer to think up letters people might write to an advice columnist and to write both questions and answers, some serious and some silly.

20. Ask the writer to name several interesting people and write about why they are interesting or how they would feel if, one day, they woke up and no longer were interesting.

Note: The idea behind this list is to suggest the number of topics for writing that young writers are surrounded by and a few of the ways you can help the child discover them.

Skills and Concepts Being Taught:

1. *Writers receive ideas for writing from the world around them*
2. *Recognizing the number of topics for writing which exist in everyday life*
3. *Responding to visual sensations with language*
4. *Imaginative thinking*
5. *Sequential thinking*

Reading List

Ages 5-6

Tales and Stories by Hans Christian Andersen

Mitsumasa Anno, *Anno's Alphabet*
Anno's Counting Book

Beshlie, *Snailsleap Lane*

Marcia Brown, *Once a Mouse*

Margaret Wise Brown, *Goodnight, Moon*

Virginia L. Burton, *The Little House*

Selina Chonz, *A Bell for Ursli*

John Ciardi, *You Read to Me, I'll Read to You*

Barbara Cooney, *Miss Rumphius*

Jean de Brunhoff, *Babar and Father Christmas*
Babar the King
The Story of Babar the Little Elephant

Virginia Hamilton, *The People Could Fly*

Randall Jarrell, *The Animal Family*
Snow White and the Seven Dwarfs, A Tale from
the Brothers Grimm

Ezra Jack Keats, *The Snowy Day*

Munro Leaf, *The Story of Ferdinand*

Arnold Lobel, *Days with Frog and Toad*
Frog and Toad All Year

Suse Macdonald, *Alphabatics*

Mercer Mayer, *The Queen Always Wanted to Dance*

Robert McClosky, *Make Way for Ducklings*

Katherine Milhous, *The Egg Tree*

Else H. Minarik, *A Kiss for Little Bear*

Beatrix Potter, *Peter Rabbit's ABC*

H. A. Rey, *Curious George*
Curious George Gets a Medal
Curious George Rides a Bike
Curious George Takes a Job

Alvin Schwartz, *In a Dark, Dark Room and Other Scary Stories*

Peter Spier, *A Book of Opposites*

William Steig, *Sylvester and the Magic Pebble*

Jeanne Titherington, *A Place for Ben*

Tasha Tudor, *1 Is One*
        A Is for Annabelle
        Around the Year

Tomi Ungerer, Crictor

Chris van Allsburg, *The Garden of Abdul Gasazi*
        The Polar Express
        The Z Was Zapped

Jan Wahl, *Humphrey's Bear*

Audrey Wood, *King Bidgood's in the Bathtub*

Taro Yashima, *Crow Boy*
        Umbrella

Ages 7-10

Verna Aardema, *Why Mosquitoes Buzz in People's Ears: A West
        African Tale*

Sholem Aleichem, *Hanukah Money*

Rebecca Caudill, *Higgins and the Great Big Scare*

Blaise Cendrars, *Shadow* (Translated and Illustrated by Marcia
        Brown)

Mark Daniel, Editor, *A Child's Treasury of Poems*

Tomie DePaola, *The Clown of God*

Barbara Emberley, *Drummer Hoff*

Nikki Giovanni, *Spin a Soft Black Song*

Rumer Godden, *The Story of Holly and Ivy*

Kenneth Grahame, *The Wind in the Willows*

Gordon Grand, *A Horse for Christmas Morning and Other Stories*

Lee B. Hopkins, *Dinosaurs*

I Like You, If You Like Me: Poems of Friendship (Macmillan
anthology)

Mavis Jukes, *Like Jake and Me*

William Kurelek, *A Prairie Boy's Winter*

Madeline L'Engle, *A Wrinkle in Time*

Rika Lesser, *Hansel and Gretel*

Arnold Lobel, *Fables*

Mirrian Mason, *Stevie and His Seven Orphans*

Gian-Carlo Menotti, *Amahl and the Night Visitors*

Alfred Ollivant, *Bob, Son of Battle*

The Random House Book of Poetry for Children

Cynthia Rylant, *The Relatives Came*

Mari Sandoz, *The Horsecatcher*

Isaac Bashevis Singer, *Naftali: The Storyteller and His Horse*

John Steinbeck, *The Red Pony*

John Steptoe, *The Story of Jumping Mouse*

Wallace Tripp, *A Great Big Ugly Man Came Up and Tied His Horse to Me: A Book of Nonsense Verse*

Chris van Allsburg, *Ben's Dream*
The Mysteries of Harris Burdick
The Stranger

E. B. White, *Charlotte's Web*
Stuart Little
The Trumpet of the Swan

Valerie Worth, *Small Poems Again*

Harve Zemach, *Duffy and the Devil*

Ages 11-14

Louisa May Alcott, *Little Men*
Little Women

C. W. Anderson, *The Blind Connemara*
The Horse of Hurricane Hill

William H. Armstrong, *Sounder*

Marion D. Bauer, *On My Honor*

Claire H. Bishop, *All Alone*

Joan Blos, *A Gathering of Days*

Frances H. Burnett, *The Secret Garden*

Sheila Burnford, *The Incredible Journey*

Betsy Byars, *A Blossom Promise*

Lewis Carroll, *Alice's Adventures in Wonderland*

G. K. Chesterton, *Father Brown Stories*

Arthur B. Chrisman, *Shen of the Sea*

Patricia Clapp, *The Tamarack Tree*

Olivia Collidge, *People in Palestine*

Susan Cooper, *The Grey King*

Eleanor Estes, *Ginger Pye*

Phyllis Fenner, *Horses, Horses, Horses*

Paula Fox, *The Slave Dancer*

Sheila Gordon, *Waiting for the Rain*

Marguerite Henry, *Misty of Chincoteague*

Annabel and Edgar Johnson, *A Memory of Dragons*

Erich Kastner, *The Little Man*

Eric Knight, *Lassie Come Home*

Joseph Krumgold, *And Now Miguel*

Jack London, *The Call of the Wild*

Jack O'Brien, *Silver Chief, Dog of the North*

Scott O'Dell, *Island of the Blue Dolphins*

Cynthia Q. Rylant, *A Fine White Dust*

Isaac Bashevis Singer, *Zlateh the Goat and Other Stories*

Robert Louis Stevenson, *Treasure Island*

Booth Tarkington, *Penrod*

Stephanie S. Tolan, *The Great Skinner Getaway*

J. R. R. Tolkien, *The Hobbit*

Cynthia Voight, *Come a Stranger*
Dicey's Song

Laura Ingalls Wilder, *The Little House in the Big Woods*

Nancy Willard, *A Visit to William Blake's Inn: Poems for Innocent
and Experienced Travelers*

Maia Wojciechowska, *Shadow of a Bull*

Chelsea Yarbro, *Floating Illusions*

Elizabeth Yates, *Amos Fortune, Free Man*

A Guide for School Teachers

Most texts on teaching writing segregate creative writing from academic writing. In *The Magic Pencil* the two types of writing are integrated, for several reasons. First, neither type is more important to children's development as writers and readers. A child who is made to feel that his or her imagination and feelings are important to others, including the teacher, does not stifle a part of himself or herself when writing or reading traditional academic material. Instead, the child who has been encouraged to express his or her feelings and imaginings in writing brings to academic writing and reading his or her whole personality and is able, then, to ask how new information or skills can be integrated into who the child is. Different types of writing become tools for the child to use in different circumstances, with the *child*, responsive to all types of writing, feeling empowered to think about who he or she wants to communicate with and what type of writing will be most appropriate. Academic writing, for such a child, ceases to be that which he or she "has" to do but, becomes, rather, a type of writing which the child seeks to do because it is appropriate as a means of communication to an envisioned audience.

In *The Magic Pencil*, children using the exercises may follow the writing of a poem with the writing of a news story or report, with both writing activities felt as creative and personal.

Second, creative and academic writing exercises are integrated to encourage children to enjoy writing and to lose a fear of failure. Children who like to write and who do so fearlessly will learn more quickly than children who find writing a chore to fear.

Third, academic and creative exercises are integrated in the text as a way to mirror how children learn in play situations, moving back and forth between trial and error and the celebration of learning which takes into account what was learned by trial and error. We have all no doubt observed a child learning to ride a bike, falling, getting up, crying, muttering, trying again; then the first triumphant, steady ride accompanied by the shout, "I can ride! Hey, look!"

Children learning to write by moving back and forth between creative and academic writing will learn to celebrate pieces of academic writing which, in images, similes, metaphors, sharp or original details, reflect a part of their personality and produce writing which is no longer "dry" and dull.

Fourth, by allowing children to move back and forth between creative and academic writing exercises, *The Magic Pencil* helps a young writer to learn to take charge of his or her writing in both forms. This, too, is similar to how children learn as they play. Sometimes children at play seek solutions for learning difficulties encountered during play and sometimes they prefer to struggle toward a solution alone. Children who are secure as they play are acknowledging that they know adult help is there if they need it; similarly, children can be secure learners of writing when the teacher allows the young writer to view the teacher as a willing guide *when* the child seeks help. Children whose emotions and imaginations are honored as frequently in creative writing exercises as their wish for logic, order, and structure are honored in academic writing exercises will genuinely feel that their teacher cares about their development and will seek guidance fearlessly when *they* feel it is needed.

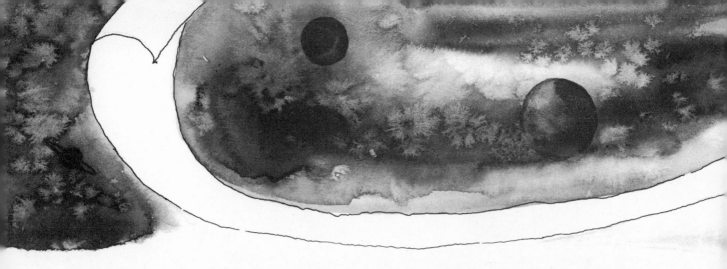

The four rationales just given for the integration of creative and academic writing exercises suggest that teachers need not fear that children do not want to become engaged in the writing process. In fact, children love to write unless they are *taught* to dislike writing. But too often children have experienced writing in school as separate from their experiences, their feelings and their sense of wonder. Instead of reaching out to learn, as children do in play, they often put up a shell of resistance to writing *because* they fear failure and because writing does not feel meaningful.

The Magic Pencil contains exercises designed specifically not only to integrate types of writing but also to combat children's fear of failure in writing.

Many of the writing exercises in *The Magic Pencil* appear to be games, and they *are* games, *serious* games involving language, form and expression. Each exercise begins with a suggestion about the teacher's role in the "game": the teacher "sets up" the "game" and then allows the children to "play."

What is required for a school teacher to use exercises in *The Magic Pencil?*

1. A teacher should feel comfortable in a bustling classroom, with children talking, writing, drawing, cutting *as* they learn.
2. A teacher should feel comfortable *not* grading every piece of writing and, in fact, evaluating children's writing by helping children learn how to evaluate their own writing.
3. A teacher should be flexible enough during a class to allow its structure to change to accommodate students' interests as they develop. In other words, a lesson in poetry writing may change into a lesson in expository writing or a lesson on writing a bibliographic entry may

turn into a lesson on storytelling. The exercises in *The Magic Pencil* can be used as examples of how set items in a curriculum can be integrated into writing exercises which free young writers to explore their imaginations *as* they learn core curriculum material.

4. A teacher should feel confident that children who enjoy writing will learn more quickly than children who feel they must write simply to satisfy a teacher's assignments.

5. A teacher should feel that *conversations* with children about writing are as important as lessons about writing during which the teacher talks and the child listens. In fact, equal conversations between child and teacher are probably more valuable.

6. A teacher should feel that creative writing and academic writing support one another and are equally important to a child's writing ability.

7. And, most importantly, a teacher using *The Magic Pencil* should be able to refrain from chastising a child for poor writing and substitute reprimand with listening: *What* is hampering the child's writing ability, and how may I better approach the child?

Gaining Confidence

Many school teachers do not feel comfortable teaching creative writing because they themselves do not write poetry or stories or plays. And their confidence may have been undermined by visiting poets or storytellers whose professional credentials as creative writers are extensive. Often visiting poets or storytellers are able to encourage children to write, joyously, wonderful stories and poems. Often they ask as the visiting writer leaves, "When can you come back?" The regular classroom teacher can feel not only inadequate but unappreciated. Yet, the visiting creative writer is no more than occasional enrichment to a writing program. Indeed, even that enrichment can be questioned pedagogically if creative writing is presented to children only as an occasional activity which must be brought into the classroom from the outside. Moreover, most visiting writers are unable to work with children over the extended period of time that would allow them to integrate creative writing into a curriculum.

It is really the classroom teacher who can best teach creative writing as a natural part of an English curriculum. And that teacher *need not be a creative writer. The Magic Pencil* provides exercises which assume that the person using them is not a practicing poet or storyteller or dramatist. The exercises focus on helping children reveal the creativity they possess naturally and on methods of encouraging that creativity. It is designed in such a way that *teachers* learn from *children* as children become involved in writing and are able to reveal to a teacher what help they seek.

Teaching creative writing to a child involves a relationship between child and teacher in which both learn about enrichment. Any teacher who loves teaching and admires his or her pupils can teach creative writing.

Afterword

Teaching kids to write is something every adult can do because kids *want* to learn to write. The only times I've seen children turn away from writing are when they have seen writing as a sure way to fail. And kids are smart: they don't want to fail. When you work with kids, let *them* guide you. Some days they won't be in the mood to write. That's fine, even though they may surprise you and participate in a prewriting activity just for fun. And some days you won't feel like teaching. That's all right, too. But your child may decide to write a story or a poem about "The Teacher Who Got Tired of Teaching One Rainy Day in March" *because* you've been teaching so well.

There are many ways to teach writing. When using *The Magic Pencil*, you may find yourself adjusting exercises to suit the child or children you're working with. And you may find yourself inventing new exercises. Or your child may begin a writing project of his or her own that takes weeks of writing. When this happens, congratulate yourself and throw the child a party!

Above all, have fun using *The Magic Pencil*. A whole world will open up for you and the children you'll teach. It can truly be magical.

Eve Shelnutt, a native of Spartanburg, South Carolina, holds a B.A. in English from the University of Cincinnati and an M.F.A. in creative writing from the University of North Carolina. Currently on the faculty of the University of Pittsburgh, she has taught creative writing to children and conducted workshops for public school teachers on teaching children to write.

She has been widely published in magazines, newspapers, and anthologies and is the author of the short story collections *The Love Child, Descant, The Formal Voice,* and *The Musician.* She is also the author of the poetry collections *Air and Salt* and *Recital in a Private Home.* Her awards for her writing include the *Mademoiselle* Fiction Award, an O. Henry Prize, the Great Lakes Fiction Award, the South Carolina Press Association Fiction Award, and the Distinguished Alumni Award from UNC. She has also been recognized with an award for Excellence in Teaching at Pitt.

Shelnutt resides in Laughlintown, Pennsylvania, with her husband and their son.

Paulette L. Lambert designs and illustrates books for several publishers. She lives in Atlanta, Georgia.